STEVE BAUGHMAN
COVER-UP IN THE KINGDOM
PHONE SEX, LIES, AND GOD'S GREAT APOLOGIST, RAVI ZACHARIAS

Cover-Up in the Kingdom: Phone Sex, Lies, And God's Great Apologist, Ravi Zacharias

Steve Baughman

ISBN (Print Edition): 978-1-54395-255-1

ISBN (eBook Edition): 978-1-54395-256-8

If the Christian faith is truly supernatural, why is it not more evident in the lives of so many Christians I know?

– An unnamed Hindu to Ravi Zacharias.[1]

ACKNOWLEDGMENTS:

"They are coming for you." So said the email I received the morning after I notified Ravi Zacharias that I had acquired a copy of the suicide threat he sent to the married woman with whom he had been having an online affair.

The Ravi Zacharias story is not pretty. There are good reasons why certain people do not want it told. But we tell it here.

I would like to thank Southern Baptist historian and archivist, Jim Lutzweiler, and Pastor Deidre Richardson of The Essential Church for encouraging me to shout this story from the rooftops. And thank you to another Baptist archivist, Bill Youngmark, and to my fellow Caribbean-born fellow skeptic, Paul Morris, for very helpful comments on the manuscript.

I would like also to acknowledge the Christian professors and activists I have worked with who have spoken out against Ravi's misconduct. In alphabetical order, Reginald Jacob Block, Tom Lunol, Dee Parsons, Dr. Randal Rauser, Julie Anne Smith, Dr. John Stackhouse, and Dr. Warren Throckmorton. These folks don't think their religion needs truth suppression to survive. So far they have been no match for HarperCollins Christian Publishing and the Southern Baptist Convention. Perhaps this book will level the playing field.

Thank you also to Serena Su Wang and Paul McCarthy for research assistance.

FOREWORD

"I promise I will leave no stone unturned in my pursuit of truth." - Ravi Zacharias, April 2018 at RZIM.org

I stumbled upon Ravi Zacharias in early 2015 as part of my ongoing attempt to stay informed about the best and the brightest defenders of the Christian faith. His impeccable credentials, which included multiple doctoral degrees as well as positions at Oxford and Cambridge, impressed me greatly. This man had the expertise to ruffle my skeptical worldview.

He also had a fondness for quoting G.K. Chesterton on truth and was himself on record time and again standing for propositions like "nothing is as important as truth"[2] and "compromising the truth is a serious blunder."[3] Ravi Zacharias was as honest as he was qualified. I wanted to learn more about him and how he defended his religious views.

My investigation took me on a most unanticipated three year journey to the dark underbelly of the Christian business world. In peeling back each layer of this charming preacher I uncovered new depths of perfidy. Ravi, it turned out, had lied for decades about his academic credentials. He had also landed himself in federal litigation over an online affair that he threatened suicide to cover up. To make matters worse, he settled that lawsuit on terms that require his victim to remain silent forever.

Most troubling was the fact that Ravi's colleagues in Christian publishing, education and ministry had long known about his many deceptions but did not seem to care. The Christian apologist and professor, Dr. John Stackhouse, told *Christianity Today* in December of 2017 that evangelicals have "quietly mentioned" Ravi's questionable credential claims for decades.[4] For some reason it took an unregenerate to cry foul.

Things got ugly quickly. In the summer of 2015, after Ravi's ministry stopped responding to my inquiries about Cambridge, I began the piecemeal process of sharing my findings with the public. Ravi's followers were not happy. And they fought back with a curiously recurring theme: they had nothing to say about my allegations, but much to say about my hating God.

In a thoughtful world we would not let messenger motives undermine the message. Sadly, that is not our world. So, for what it's worth, here goes. I actually do not hate God, nor do I hate religion. And although I do not believe there is a God to hate (or to love) I know many brilliant scholars who think I am demonstrably wrong about this. This works as a check against excessive skeptical cockiness on my part. When I find myself rolling my eyes at a religious claim I will often stop to ask myself "WWAPD?" ("What would Alvin Plantinga do?") The knowledge that I could be wrong about religion is what led me to Ravi Zacharias.

Those who view my Ravi work as just another skeptic wanting to take down an effective man of God will perhaps not notice that I speak no ill of the N.T. Wrights, Peter van Inwagens, Eleonore Stumps and Anselm Ramelows of the world. These Christian scholars do not need fake credentials and sophomoric sleight-of-hand arguments to defend their religion. They are the real deal. Ravi Zacharias isn't.

I am struck by the frequency with which Ravi's defenders insist that he has responded thoroughly to the sex and credential fraud allegations. He has not. As this book goes to print, Ravi has not publicly commented on the suicide threat he made to cover up his online affair. Nor has he explained the false claims he made for many years about Cambridge, Oxford and Alliance Theological Seminary. He has also failed to address his decades long resistance to using the word "honorary" when telling the world about his doctorate degrees. His ministry, for its part, evaded questions about hush money payments. The fact is that, far from facing the allegations, Ravi has been evasive, crafty and dishonest in his response to the growing pile of evidence of misconduct on his part. And although his evasion is in the public record his defenders still claim that he has "put to rest" all these troubling matters.[5] One cannot but wonder what this says about the ability of many evangelical Christians to process unpleasant information.

I wrote this book for two reasons. First, and uncontroversial, if Christians want to compete in the marketplace of ideas they must do so without resorting to false pretenses. Ravi Zacharias has too long been an imposter in the hallowed dialogue between skeptics and the religious. His shortcut-to-certainty mindset has fueled what Biola's Craig Hazen calls the "growth industry" of Christian apologetics, which I consider a dangerous (though probably fun) exercise in dumbing down complexity. A Zacharias Academy certificate (or a Biola Master's Degree in Christian Apologetics, for that matter) might teach you to win a verbal bar fight, but if you wish to go up against a true martial artist, or simply to find an honest intellectual peace, you must spend decades in the temple. Ravi's greatest intellectual sin has not been his dishonesty but his shallowness. There is a rich discussion underway between committed scholars on all sides of the God issues. Ravi Zacharias muddies the water with his pretended expertise. May this book nudge him aside with speed.

Second, a theological point. I consider it fair fighting to suggest that if Christianity were true, Christians would be different. The religion's official documents speak mightily of the sanctifying power of the blood of Jesus. This is one of the few testable claims Christianity makes. If being a "new creature" in Christ means anything, it means being significantly different from us old creatures. If Jesus really sanctifies we should see more than mere anecdotes about lost wretches getting found; we should see vast differences between God, Inc. and Tobacco, Inc.

A Hindu once asked Ravi "If the Christian faith is truly supernatural, why is it not more evident in the lives of so many Christians I know?"[6]

Perhaps this heathen had a premonition about something that is now more widely known; Ravi Zacharias's secret life is a counterexample to the message of his public life. Of course, a single failure of a miracle drug does not make it snake oil. But when the industry leaders who push the miracle drug do not bother taking it, or they take it to no effect, critics are not unreasonable to view that as weighing against the miraculousness of the drug.

In this book we shall see that significant parts of the Christian business world (here I refer to seminaries, colleges, evangelical organizations, churches and publishers) have not manifested the newness that the religion of their livelihoods promises. To what extent that undermines the truth of the world's biggest religion is, I submit, a legitimate point for discussion.

Thoughtful readers will spare me the "Christians aren't perfect, just forgiven" straw man. No skeptic worth her salt considers the absence of perfect Christians to be evidence against the truth of the religion. The claim is, rather, that if Christianity were true, Christians would be noticeably different around the things that matter, like money and integrity in business. They aren't. Therefore, . . .

Whatever one thinks of my theological point, the machinations of Ravi Zacharias and the response of Christian business interests to these provide us a valuable learning opportunity. It is my privilege now to share the results of my three year investigations of "the great apologist of our time"[7] and of those who enable him.

CHAPTER 1: A SHATTERED FACADE

"Are you going to tell him it's me?" - Ravi Zacharias to Lori Anne Thompson on October 29, 2016. (Appendix 2.)

A lifetime of public ministry will never reveal as much about the character of evangelist Ravi Zacharias as do the eight words he penned at 4:38 p.m. on October 29, 2016. The man known as "the great apologist of our time" had been a pretender for thirty five years. He was about to get caught.

In 2014 Ravi Zacharias began having an online relationship with a married Canadian woman. While at times I use the word "affair" to describe the relationship, this is only a matter of shorthand. The power imbalance between Ravi and Lori Anne Thompson likely made the dynamic more of a manipulative "grooming" process by the wealthy celebrity. Fortunately, we need not speculate about this. We know that the relationship soon turned sexual. Ravi requested and began receiving sexual photos from Lori Anne. When the pangs of conscience overtook her she informed him by email that the relationship was over. That night she would tell her husband.[8]

Ravi panicked and sent Lori Anne the two emails that will become his most lasting legacy. The renowned preacher who traveled the world railing against atheist immorality told Ms. Thompson in writing that if she took the step that was so necessary to healing her marriage he would kill himself. That was October, 2016.

On the afternoon of November 28, 2017, I informed Ravi and his ministry that I had acquired a copy of his suicide threat. The next morning

I received an email from a source I did not recognize. The subject was "look out". I opened it and saw these words: "They are coming for you and u need to tell whoever is your source that also." [9]

Ravi may have had nothing to do with this threat. But he had good reason to panic. His life was, by all accounts, an impressive tale of success. Since graduating from seminary in 1976 he had built a vast empire of evangelical organizations bearing his name. His flagship entity, Ravi Zacharias International Ministries (RZIM), had offices in 16 countries and in 2016, the year of his suicide threat, brought in $42,000,000 in donations.[10] He was an award winning author with some twenty books to his credit and more on the way. His weekly radio show reached more than 2000 outlets. Ravi was also about to open yet another eponymous ministry, The Zacharias Institute, which he promised donors would be the "leading apologetics center in the world."[11]

Ravi's assures us that his habit of naming supposedly Christ-focused organizations after himself had nothing to do with ego. Perhaps he was a little uncomfortable with the optics of it all for he tells us in his memoirs how RZIM got its name:

> I had proposed a different name for the ministry other than my own name, but after everyone pondered it overnight, they advised, "No, Ravi, so much has happened with people in ministry having gone astray. If you give this ministry your name, it will stand up behind your integrity, or fall with the lack of it."[12]

Ravi's suicide emails to Lori Anne Thompson were not the only things that threatened to make the falling part of that prophecy come true. It had already been a dangerous eighteen months of dodging reputational bullets for the evangelist regarded by so many as God's best line of defense against the secular onslaught in the academy. In May of 2015 we learned that "Dr. Zacharias" had employed misleading language in his official bio to conceal the fact that he had no academic doctorates. The next month the University of Cambridge confirmed that he had never been a "visiting scholar" at their institution, a claim he had widely made in writings and lecturers. The University of Oxford then confirmed that Ravi's claims to have been a professor and "an official lecturer" at their institution were false.

It kept coming. In early 2017 Cambridge confirmed that the professor Ravi said he studied quantum physics under in 1990, John Polkinghorne, had not taught physics that year at all. Then came the revelation that the "department" Ravi said he chaired at Alliance Theological Seminary never existed.

Ravi began to remove misleading claims from his website and press materials. It was the honest thing to do, but that he was able to get away with these deceptions for decades points to a difference between the values of the God business and those of its worldly counterpart. When Penguin Books discovered significant deceptions in Margaret Seltzer's *Love and Consequences* it recalled all copies and canceled her book tour.[13] When Knopf Doubleday discovered "that a number of facts have been altered and incidents embellished" in James Frey's *A Million Little Pieces* it refused to fulfill new orders until changes were made.[14] Oprah berated Mr. Frey so fiercely on her show that had it been a boxing match they would have stopped the fight. Jon Krakauer created a small cottage industry from the outrage over the falsehoods in Greg Mortenson's *Three Cups of Tea*.[15]

But in the Christian business world the operative principle has long been that if it helps the bottom line it probably also helps the Kingdom.[16]

Ravi flourished not despite his deceptions, but because of them.

But this time it was different. This time it was about sex.

CHAPTER 2: SEX, SUICIDE
AND LITIGATION

"When one of you has a dispute with another believer, how dare you file a lawsuit and ask a secular court to decide the matter instead of taking it to other believers? ... Why not just accept the injustice and leave it at that?"
- Romans Chapter 6.

Two years before Ravi's suicide threat he had met Lori Anne at a ministry function in Ontario, Canada. It was October 3, 2014.[17] She was a slight blonde with a heart full of compassion, and eyes that communicated it.[18] They began emailing and the evangelist soon desired to communicate with her about matters that required an encrypted method of communication. By his own admission, Ravi asked Lori Anne, a woman he hardly knew, to communicate with him via his private Blackberry address.[19] In the course of their online relationship (the two were never alone together) Ravi requested and received nude and sexual photos from her.[20]

By late October of 2016, the "soul searing shame" of marital deceit had taken its toll on Lori Anne. On October 29 at 1:04 p.m. she emailed Ravi. "I can no longer continue, even in the seams of my soul, tuck away what I know to be a sin against God and each of our spouses."[21] Tonight, "in order to move forward with my spouse," she said, she would tell Brad.[22] Ravi's secret was about to break.

Writer Robert McKee may as well have had Ravi Zacharias in mind when he said, "True character is revealed in the choices a human being makes under pressure - the greater the pressure, the deeper the revelation, the truer the choice to the character's essential nature."[23] Fifty years of bathing in the sanctifying blood of Christ and in that pressure-packed moment the great evangelist could not muster up enough integrity to meet even the most minimal standards of decency. Ravi abandoned all godly pretenses and showed Lori Anne who he really was. And he did so in writing.

At 4:38:48 p.m., a mere 48 seconds after asking Lori Anne if she planned to disclose his identity to her husband, Ravi Zacharias threatened suicide:

"You promised you wouldn't Lori Anne. If. You betray me here I will have no option but to bid this world goodbye I promise." [sic].[24]

Lori Anne called his bluff. She told Brad. And Ravi broke his promise. Instead of killing himself he went full force into damage control mode. What ensued was a few weeks of three anguished adults working out their issues by email.

Brad wrote to Ravi "I cannot express enough my wish for restoration for you especially your heart as I too am a man just like you who has lived to [sic] long in his head."[25] Lori Anne told Ravi, "I will cover you with a blanket of mercy now and always and ask that you do the same for me."[26]

Ravi "sobbed [his] heart out" over the reconciliation. "[W]e sing so much about Grace," he wrote to the couple, "but there is nothing like being on the receiving end when it is a pure gift and completely undeserved by the recipient."[27]

The cyber-warmth soon faded. On December 5, Brad wrote Ravi for assurances that the "clothed and nude" photos had been destroyed. Lori Anne, he noted, had inquired of Ravi about this earlier but had received no reply. Ravi assured Brad that all photos had been destroyed "within seconds" and that he would be giving up the use of a cell phone, "shattering this one and therefore unlocatable or unusable to self or anyone."[28]

At that point, the available email record went dark. What happened next may be lost to history. But out of that darkness there emerged a much darker record, a detailed public record created by lawyers for the parties in federal action 17-cv-02885-LMM, <u>Ravi Zacharias vs. Bradley and Lori Anne Thompson</u>.

On April 27, 2017, Ravi received a letter marked "Personal and Extremely Confidential" from Mark Bryant, an attorney representing the Thompsons.[29] It contained nothing surprising, just another familiar allegation that a powerful man of God had behaved in a sexually abusive manner with a younger woman not his wife. The letter described in detail how Ravi used his grooming skills to establish a confidential relationship of spiritual trust with Lori Anne and then used her for his own sexual satisfaction. Ravi Zacharias, per the letter, had committed multiple acts of marital infidelity and clergy misconduct with this lawyer's client. To make matters worse, the lawyer had the emails and a call register to prove it. He also had a copy of Ravi's suicide email.

Then, in what looked like blackmail, Mark Bryant demanded $5,000,000 to forego "public litigation." It was a most indelicate bit of lawyering. But blackmail or not, Ravi had much to hide. And desperate times require desperate measures. Ravi took the initiative. On July 31, 2017 he sued the Thompsons.

How is it that so gifted a preacher as Ravi Zacharias fell into the risky behavior that landed him in such legal and professional jeopardy? It is tempting to blame the usual suspect, libido. However, something more is at work here.

A common thread underlies the risks Ravi took with Lori Anne and the ones he took with his brazenly fabricated academic credentials. Since his early days as an ordained preacher, Ravi has flirted with deception, and thus with disaster. Why? Has the God he so eloquently proclaims as his savior not been enough to keep his life interesting?

Perhaps there is within Ravi Zacharias a still small voice that calls for others to look past the success object and see that lonely teenager who, as we shall see, went from attempted suicide to stardom so quickly that he bypassed real recovery and growth. Each new round of risk taking is a cry; "Please! I am not who you think I am!" His latest cry is the loudest so far. And it is very loud indeed.

The folks in the God business who surround Ravi cannot let themselves notice. That would cost them dearly. In the eyes and interests of HarperCollins Christian Publishing, Ravi Zacharias is the beautiful whore, or at least the useful holy man, who must, at all cost, be kept at work.

But the rainmaking preacher now stands on the precipice of crashing failure, all brought about by his own haphazard approach to matters of integrity and truth. A powerful religious industrial complex stands by his side, determined to keep him from falling. Will they succeed? Probably not. But let us approach that precipice and see how it is that the great apologist of our time has come to stand so close to its edge.

CHAPTER 3: EARLY TROUBLES, GOD'S POISON, AND FINDING RELIGION

"One of the most emphasized lessons I learned from listening all around and observing was that you had to succeed professionally. Keep your private heartache private; keep your collapsing world propped up. Professional appearance is all that you could take with you." - Ravi Zacharias memoirs.[30]

Understanding Ravi's childhood makes it hard not to have compassion for him. It also makes it hard not to see through him.

He spent his first twenty years in India with a cruel and violent father who beat him, ridiculed him, and convinced him that he was going nowhere in life. In his memoirs, *Walking from East to West*, Ravi speaks movingly of a deep sense of inferiority and intense loneliness that "stemmed from the fact that all my friends were either rich or brilliant, and I was neither."[31] In those pages he speaks also of "the inner struggle of my soul" and of his "need to act like I really was somebody." [32]

For Ravi Zacharias it has always been about how he stacks up against others. "I was the one among our band of friends who had the least promise of a future."[33] And it did not help that he was surrounded by high-achievers, his father, his older brother, his friends, and the "distinguished gene pool"[34] that his family had been blessed with. Their blessedness was but a curse to the young Ravi desperately craving respect.

Ravi's obsession with celebrity and success is the most prominent theme in his memoirs and in his later promotional materials. These words are from his official bio shortly prior to the credentials scandal:

HEAR
Ravi
Zacharias
"THE
BILLY GRAHAM OF INDIA"
As he returns from a great
Crusade in Cambodia and Israel.

MAY WE HELP YOU? We can if
you come out to hear Ravi
Zacharias, the Billy Graham of India, March 19 to 26 at First Alliance Church, 111 Mission Meade
Drive. No fee, just call 654-4512 or
654-5103.

PRESENTING
INDIA'S FUTURE BILLY GRAHAM

RAVI ZACHARIAS

This 32-year-old evangelist has been called
to preach and he does so with a prophetic
voice and a note of authority." —Dr. Paul
Smith, pastor Peoples Church, Toronto,
Ontario

For More Information Call
654-4512 or 654-5193
Rev. M. E. Nicholson, Pastor

RAVI ZACHARIAS

The Tampa Tribune (Tampa, FL), July 27, 1974 (top). New Castle News (New Castle, PA),
March 15, 1978 (middle). New Castle News (New Castle, PA), March 18, 1978 (bottom).

Dr. Zacharias has spoken all over the world for 43 years in scores of universities, notably Harvard, Dartmouth, Johns Hopkins, and Oxford University. He has addressed writers of the peace accord in South Africa, the president's cabinet and parliament in Peru, and military officers at the Lenin Military Academy and the Center for Geopolitical Strategy in Moscow. At the invitation of the President of Nigeria, he addressed delegates at the First Annual Prayer Breakfast for African Leaders held in Mozambique.

Dr. Zacharias has direct contact with key leaders, senators, congressmen, and governors who consult him on an ongoing basis. He has addressed the Florida Legislature and the Governor's Prayer Breakfast in Texas and Louisiana, and has twice spoken at the Annual Prayer Breakfast at the United Nations in New York, which marks the beginning of the UN General Assembly each year. As the 2008 Honorary Chairman of the National Day of Prayer, he gave addresses at the White House, the Pentagon, and The Cannon House. He has had the privilege of addressing the National Prayer Breakfasts in the seats of government in Ottawa, Canada, and London, England, and speaking at the CIA in Washington, DC.[35]

Clearly, this is not a man with much interest in the kinds of people Jesus consorted with. It is hard to picture the eponymous empire-building Ravi Zacharias accepting an assignment to live among lepers even if the command came from On High. Ravi "jumped at the chance" to meet celebrities[36] and he makes it clear that from the beginning his eyes were on high places of the worldly sort. Ravi was determined from the moment of his conversion to become as Billy Graham as possible.[37]

Nobody deserves blame for not wanting to be an apostle to the lepers. Still, with all the time Ravi spent in India one might expect that he would have had at least one meaningful encounter with a named poor person. But he never did. Or if he did it was not meaningful enough to deserve a place in his memoirs. Those pages are reserved primarily for film stars, sports heroes, generals, politicians, wealthy donors, exotic and courageous missionaries and the evangelical glitterati, and also for the Ravi Zacharias exploits that remind us that, despite a rough start, he is to be counted among their number.

Ravi assures us that he really did care about the poor. In the opening pages of his memoirs he tells us that he would return to India from time to time with some money for the less fortunate, who responded with a moving appreciation.[38] He also lets us know about the charitable work he does for sex abuse victims and the destitute through RZIM Wellspring International.[39] Yes, Ravi Zacharias cares about the poor. But he leaves no doubt as to where his passions are. What Saul of Tarsus was to the gentiles, Ravi Zacharias wanted to be to the stars.[40]

Unfortunately, as a teenager he was no star. And the failure got to be too much. At age 17 Ravi decided to end his life. He tells us that he was neither depressed nor impulsive and he gives no indication that he was tormented by his sinful nature. On the contrary, Ravi's suicide decision was a cool business calculation. Life was a zero-sum game and others gaining meant he was left behind. "Everyone else around me had success, but no matter how deeply I searched my life for a shred of it, all I saw was failure."[41] A quiet exit, he decided, "will spare me any further failure."[42]

One day when his family was away Ravi locked himself in his bathroom, took poison and wound up on the floor in danger of dying. Two things saved his life. First, the Lord made sure he took the "right poison."[43] Second, and secondarily, Ravi's family had a house servant who was working in the kitchen that day. When this man heard Ravi cry for help he "banged hard" on the bathroom door as Ravi lay incapacitated on the floor. He then "burst through, snapping the door off its hinges." Inside the bathroom he saw the urgency of the situation his young master was in.

This house servant acted with great dispatch to get Ravi to the doctors who helped him overcome the life-threatening effects of God's chosen poison. This man then cleaned up the mess in the bathroom so as to protect Ravi from the embarrassment and shame of having made a suicide attempt.[44]

This man saved Ravi's life.

This man's name was house servant.[45]

Someone with three dimensions entered Ravi's life a few days later. Fred Davis was part Anglo, the director of Youth for Christ in Delhi, energetic with "a rich baritone voice and he usually led the music at the YFC gatherings, accompanying himself on the accordion."[46] Fred stopped by the hospital to pass on a Bible and some spiritual instructions. Nothing heroic, but he was a man of position.

Ravi got saved and began to experience a renewed love of life. Once "a creature of despair, irresponsibility, and failure," he quickly became "a creature of hope, diligent and accomplished in the things to which I set my hand." "The reversal was staggering." This could only have been "the work of God."[47]

Religious conversions are often presented this way. But peel away the "saved a wretch like me" dogma and we should expect to find something far less mysterious at work, something that has little to do with the healing power of the blood of Christ. Ravi's salvation fit the mold.

Ravi, remember, was never bothered by his sinful nature. He was bothered by his mediocrity. Very, very bothered. Now suddenly he was special. His religious conversion brought him into the vibrant YFC scene that "gave me opportunities for leadership."[48] He quickly became active in "preaching and outreach".[49] The YFC leaders, he tells us, "saw something in me."[50] He was soon recruited by local leaders to "organize a good gathering" for the India YFC leader who was coming to town.[51]

Ravi was becoming a somebody. The troubled young man who "profoundly" wanted "to be needed" in the church was getting what he wanted, at last.[52] In a moment of unguarded disclosure, he tells us, "It wasn't the church so much that spawned my growth as it was the Youth for Christ environment."[53] The YFC folks around him delivered the feeling of special-ness he needed.

Ravi quickly exploited this welcoming environment for the boost it conferred on his still fragile self-image. In what he next encountered Ravi found the *modus operandi* that would launch his career and that, to this day, keeps him on the road many months a year.

CHAPTER 4: THE CROSS OR THE STAGE?

"From the very beginning . . . I knew I wanted to preach." - Ravi Zacharias[54]

Was it the love of the gospel that motivated Ravi? Or the rush of sharing it? He gives us a refreshingly uncensored answer in his memoirs.

In 1965 Ravi was asked to participate in a Youth for Christ preaching contest in Hyderabad. He tells us in his published writings that it was an international competition,[55] but in this he misleads. I contacted the three judges he mentions in his memoirs and learned that it was an India-only competition.[56] One of them also told me, "As a young man going around the world I was just asked to judge this little contest."[57] Ravi's flamboyant description of contestants gathering "from all across India and Asia"[58] is another of the self-serving exaggerations we will see so many of in this book.

Even so, it was a life changing event for the ambitious young man looking for a way to make his mark on the world. It was here that Ravi first truly feasted on the drug that would sustain him in his struggle with the demons of inferiority.

<u>Hyderabad 1965</u>

During the first round of the contest Ravi preached on "The Love of God." Here is what he tells us happened when he was done.

> Once I finished my buddies gathered around, wide-eyed. "Ravi, we're proud of you." "That was a moving sermon." "God's hand was on you." Fred Davis was like a big brother with his arm around me:

"The Lord had a purpose in this man! Thanks for your courage. God will honor you."[59]

When Ravi won the next round "my buddies went crazy. I was numb - utterly numb - and overcome with emotion."[60] Sam Kamalesan, who was one of the judges and, Ravi tells us, "probably the best-known Indian Christian at that time," said "I think we are seeing a young man today whom God has put his hand on."[61]

Ravi won the final round, and at the end of his sermon "young people streamed forward to make their own commitments."[62] He was given what he calls the "Asian Youth Preacher Award," an impressive sounding prize that curiously appears nowhere except in connection with Ravi Zacharias.[63]

On the train ride back home Ravi marveled at how he had come "from being nothing, a nobody, to being listened to by so many in different walks of life."[64] Decades later he would write about the "special sensation" he had experienced when he preached in those early days.[65]

Ravi's need for adulation is a constant theme throughout his career. Nearly two decades after Hyderabad he would speak in Amsterdam to four thousand ministers whom he tells us had been described as "the cream of the world's evangelists." Ravi writes of the "sheer exhilaration" he experienced preaching to that group and of the "affirmations that came from some of the finest people whom I admired."[66] And forty years after Hyderabad Ravi describes in detail the "tremendous" response he received to a lecture he gave to a Christian group at Harvard in 1993: "Each time I finished, students and faculty stood to their feet and applauded. It had a profound impact on those who were there."[67]

It was Hyderabad 1965 where Ravi Zacharias discovered the drug he needed to ward off suicidal feelings, loneliness and his deep seated sense of inferiority. It was not the Lord, it was the stage. And it worked.

Drugs, however, eventually wear off. This one was no exception.

CHAPTER 5: "GO WEST, YOUNG MAN!" THE DECEPTION BEGINS

"Eloquence, when at its highest pitch, leaves little room for reason or reflection." - David Hume in "Of Miracles," in *An Enquiry Concerning Human Understanding.*

For some reason God wanted the newly regenerate Ravi Zacharias to leave India for Canada. That is to say, God wanted Ravi as far away as earthly possible from the truly destitute people dying every day in the streets of Delhi with no loving hand to guide them to salvation.

The Canadian ambassador had offered to help Ravi's father move the family to Canada.[68] Ravi felt "sheer excitement" [69] at the prospect and immediately concluded that it must be the Lord's will. If God wanted Ravi to leave India for one of the finest dwelling spots on the planet, Ravi would boldly go.[70]

A lot of Eastern holy men, as well as engineers and Bollywood actors, get such instructions from On High. "Go West, with a capital W, young man!" One might be tempted to speculate that if the invite had come from the Rwandan ambassador, Ravi would have done more divine due diligence. We will never know.

In any event the extreme brevity of Ravi's thought process around the decision to leave impoverished India for comfortable Canada tells us much about his priorities. In the 1960's Christians made up a mere 2.4% of India's population. According to a 2015 Pew Research Center report that percentage is expected to drop to 2.2 percent by 2050. Catholics are largest of India's Christians groups.[71]

Ravi's home in Alpharetta, GA. Photo by Jim Lutzweiler. According to Zillow the 4,900 sq ft house has a one year projected value of $700,000.

If my calculations are correct then, this means that the number of unsaved souls in India exceeds the entire population of the United States, Canada and Europe combined. But God's ways are not ours and He wanted Ravi to leave India.

It was May of 1966.[72] Ravi and his brother, Ajit, made the move ahead of the rest of the family. In Toronto Ravi pursued what had been a long standing interest in hotel and restaurant management. But "maximizing margins" and "figuring out ways to sell more food and liquor" quickly lost its allure.[73] He continued to long for the special sensation that preaching had given him.[74]

Soon Ravi was taking classes at the Toronto Baptist Seminary. He later enrolled in the Ontario Bible College and received a Bachelor's Degree in theology. He then completed a Masters of Divinity at Trinity Evangelical

Divinity School in Illinois.[75] This is the full extent of Ravi Zacharias's completed post-high school education.

Let us pause here for a moment and settle two matters of later controversy in Ravi's life. First, Trinity is a very well-regarded seminary that has a rigorous M.Div. program. But its M.Div. is and always has been a professional degree, not an academic one.[76] Thus, for all the hullabaloo about "Dr. Zacharias's" academic credentials one thing is certain; Ravi Zacharias has no academic credentials beyond his Bachelor's degree in theology.[77]

Second, for all the tales of the fearless apologist locking horns with scholarly atheist foes,[78] Ravi Zacharias has completed only degrees with evangelical Christian professors whose job it was to help him believe more strongly what he already believed. The great apologist has actually played it intellectually safe all along. And his safe harbor existence continues to this day as he refuses to debate skeptics one-on-one. Ravi only engages opponents in his post-lecture Q&A sessions where he controls the microphone and the agenda or, pen in hand, from the safety of his study.[79]

Now back on track. Ravi graduated from Trinity in 1976[80] and began a period of international and itinerant preaching. In 1980 he took a teaching job at the Alliance Theological Seminary in Nyack, New York (hereafter ATS.) The seminary was operated by the denomination Ravi had chosen to join, the Christian and Missionary Alliance.

Ravi tells us nothing of the contract negotiations between himself and the seminary. Nor should he. But what I learned about those negotiations gives us an important insight into how this very ambitious man operated behind the scenes very early in his career.

Ravi's private business dealings with ATS tell us that the adoring crowds like those of Hyderabad 1965 would no longer do the trick. Ravi was about to take his first job in an academic atmosphere. As an academic he would need to be more than a master of divinity and stagecraft. He would need scholarly credentials. But he had none. So, as addicts are wont to do, he resorted to extreme measures to get what he craved. In those very early years at ATS Ravi fell into deception in the service of his public image. And this descent is documented in a personnel file that to this day sits with the human resources director at the seminary in Nyack. Let us take a look.

CHAPTER 6: RAVI'S FIRST PUBLIC LIE: DEPARTMENT CHAIR AT ALLIANCE THEOLOGICAL SEMINARY

"Lie not to one another." - Colossians 3:9.

What happened at Alliance Theological Seminary in the 1980's may seem far removed from the real-life issues that now interest us about Ravi Zacharias. But the records from those years, which include Ravi's personnel file at the seminary, show us that deception was part of his self-promotion even in the very early stages of his career. Ravi's post-scandal attempts to paint himself as a humble man constantly vigilant about accuracy in his C.V. count on nobody ever bothering to look at his Alliance seminary years.

Ravi's first act of blatant public deception was to refer to himself as the chair of a department that did not exist. It was a brazen move, but one that his Christian colleagues let slide. He began teaching at the small seminary in 1980. While there Ravi became the chair of something called the "Center for Evangelism and Contemporary Thought."[81]

As those in academia know, being the chair of a "center" can be a prestigious position, or a very modest one. Anyone can start a center, group, club or committee, and make themselves its chair. By stark contrast, being a *department* chair requires, first, an existing academic department and, second, a formal academic appointment to the chair of that department.

Ravi's center was on the modest end of the spectrum, to put it charitably. I tracked down three of his ATS colleagues from the 1980's and each

described the "center" to me as an informal undertaking. An ATS professor from that time, now the president of a large seminary, said it was "not
a center in terms of a think tank, more of an opportunity for students to
work with Ravi."[82]

● **Guest Speaker** at Faith Presbyte-
rian Church, 720 Marsh Road, Carrcroft,
will be the Rev. Dr. Ravi Zacharius, chairman of the department of evangelism
and contemporary thought at Alliance
Theological Seminary in Nyack, N.Y., at
11 a.m. and 7 p.m.

The News Journal (Wilmington, DE) December 04, 1982

Needing better credentials, in around 1982 Ravi simply began to refer
to the center as a "department" and to describe himself as "the chairman
of the *Department* of Evangelism and Contemporary Thought" at ATS.[83]

It smelled fishy to me. As department chair Ravi would have been in
a position of authority over some accomplished academics with far better
credentials than his own. Was he qualified for such a position?

It turns out that there were no departments at ATS. It was too small
a school.[84] Just as he had done with the "Asian Youth Preacher Award,"
Ravi simply invented the "department of Evangelism and Contemporary
Thought." And although he made the false claim publicly while he was still
at the seminary, none of his Christian colleagues called him on it, at least
not publicly.

But there was more. As early as 1981 Ravi billed himself as a "professor of contemporary thought."[85] I was puzzled by the "contemporary
thought" in this title. Evangelism might be a soft field about persuasion
and pulpit tricks, but "contemporary thought" involves the formidable and
intellectually demanding field of philosophy. Did Ravi have the qualifications for this title?

On May 3, 2017, I contacted ATS Human Resources director, Karen Davie, by email and inquired about Ravi's titles. She informed me in writing that Ravi's contractual titles with the Seminary were, first, "Chair and Associate Professor of Evangelism," and then later "Adjunct Associate Professor of Evangelism."[86]

Where was "contemporary thought"?

I spoke to Ms. Davie the next day on the phone. She told me that she had Ravi's personnel file before her and that there was "a story" there. I then learned that this file contained long buried evidence of the manipulative behavior that the status-obsessed young preacher had resorted to in private in order to further his public image.

Ms. Davie proceeded to tell me that it had been "important to Ravi" to have the words "contemporary thought" in his title but that the seminary president had not approved of this. The president, she said, "was concerned about how this would look to others." She directed me to a school catalogue that listed Ravi as an "Associate Professor of Evangelism and Contemporary Thought,"[87] but told me that this title that did not properly reflect the president's wishes. Ravi's contractual title simply did not contain the words "contemporary thought."

How did Ravi get into the school catalogue with this more prestigious title that he never held? What was going on here?

I attempted to follow up, but on May 12, 2017, I received an email from ATS general counsel, Walter Sevastian, asking me to refrain from further contacting ATS employees. When I then directed my inquiries to him he replied saying that the school "will take no position or issue any further comment on this matter."[88] He did, however, direct me to the catalogue showing Ravi as an Associate Professor of Evangelism and Contemporary Thought, the same title Ms. Davie had told me the president did not approve of. He informed me that this was Ravi's title.

The seminary's general counsel was now contradicting its human resources director, the one with Ravi's file right in front of her! When I pointed this out to Mr. Sevastian, he had no comment.

Is there an unpleasant backstory here? Ravi left the seminary after four years. He tells us he left on his own accord because he had a burning desire to preach Jesus.[89] Is that true? Or were there other reasons for his departure from ATS?

Because the C&MA keeps the records, we may never know. But two things are certain; first, as a new preacher Ravi Zacharias was already jockeying behind the scenes and pushing ethical boundaries on behalf of his public image.

Second, there is a large file with a Ravi Zacharias "story" in it sitting at the Christian and Missionary Alliance seminary in Nyack, New York. Every day that the C&MA keeps it under lock and key and refuses comment about Ravi Zacharias is another day of collusion with a deceptive man who is the denomination's most prominent evangelist.[90]

Had Ravi's colleagues at the C&MA summoned a modicum of courage to gently inform the young preacher that Christians take credential puffing seriously, Ravi's life may have taken a different course. This would have been costly to him, and perhaps to the C&MA. A Ravi Zacharias without impressive academic qualifications would not have been able to work his way into the public imagination as God's apologist to the academy.

For better or worse, it seems that nobody gave him such counsel. Instead, the lesson to Ravi Zacharias was one of tolerance for deception in God's service. It was a lesson on which he quickly capitalized.

Dr. Ravi Zacharias,
Professor of Contemporary Thought,
Alliance Theological Seminary

ANNIVERSARY EASTER SERVICES
with Dr. Ravi Zacharias

Dr. Ravi Zacharias
"THE BIBLE & MODERN MAN"
6:00 P.M. — Fellowship Supper
at Brookside Community Club

SPEAKER: RAVI ZACHARIAS D. D.

Dealing with Such Contemporary and Thought Provoking Issues as:
—Where is the Church at the End of the 20th Century?
—What is the Relevance of the Church:
—In an Age of Uncertainty—
—In an Age of Conflict—
—Where Are We in the Decade after the Death of God?

● *The PUBLIC IS INVITED TO ATTEND ANY AND ALL SERVICES -
NO CHARGE*

For More Information. Call 753-7511

Ravi has ministered extensively around the world. He is an International Evangelist with the Christian and Missionary Alliance. The unique aspect of this ministry is not limited to effectiveness in the local church, but also includes ministry to the secular mind in a pluralistic society. He is well versed in the fields of comparative religion, cults, and secular philosophies.
Ravi currently holds the chair of Evangelism and ContemporaryThought at the Alliance Theological Seminary, Nyack, New York.

Ravi Zacharias

(Sources, top to button) The Journal News (Westchester, NY) November 28, 1981.
The Gazette (Montreal, Canada) April 3, 1982. The Daily Record (Morristown,
NJ) March 06, 1982. Longview New Journal (Longview, TX) April 20, 1984

CHAPTER 7: "DR. ZACHARIAS" I AM NOT A DOCTOR BUT I PLAY ONE IN REAL LIFE

"Ravi personally does not brandish his credentials and routinely asks not to be referred to as 'Dr. Zacharias'—even by employees…" - RZIM press release, December 3, 2017.[91]

"Dr. Zacharias's office" - Ravi's personal secretary answering the phone in late 2015.

EIGHT - The number of references to "Dr. Zacharias" in Ravi's 2015 bio. (Appendix 7.)

The rules around use of the title "Dr." by people who have only honorary doctorates are clear and commonsensical; thou shalt not mislead.[92]

Ravi misled. He misled early. He misled often. And he misled systematically. To make matters worse, when he was caught misleading in 2017, he and his ministry misled to cover it up. These are strong claims. But if anyone has doubts about the deceptive intentions of Ravi Zacharias and the willingness of his ministry to further mislead in covering up his falsehoods, a quick look at how he misused his honorary doctorates will put these to rest. Let us take a look.

In 1980 the small Christian school, Houghton College, awarded Ravi his first honorary doctorate.[93] Ravi soon began to use the title "Dr. Zacharias" or simply "Ravi Zacharias. D.D." (Doctor of Divinity) in his promotional materials.[94] "Dr. Zacharias" later became ubiquitous in his books, videos and YouTube videos. Sometimes he simply said that he "holds three doctorates."[95] By 2015, when I began investigating him, his official bio at RZIM referred to him as "Dr. Zacharias" eight times in its descriptions of his accomplishments.[96]

Although at times Ravi disclosed that his doctorates were honorary,[97] for the most part he assiduously avoided using the word "honorary" in his bio and publicity materials.[98] More deviously, in his official website bio he described his doctorates in language that was not only ambiguous but identical to the language used by a large university in describing its Ph.D. students. Ravi said he had been "honored with the conferring of" various doctoral degrees.[99] This is the same language that Ohio State University uses for its engineering students who will soon be conferred academic doctorates.[100]

I called Ravi in late 2015 at his headquarters and was transferred to his personal secretary. She answered by announcing that this was "Dr. Zacharias's office."

It was a great surprise, therefore, to see Ravi and his ministry claim in their much anticipated December, 2017 press release that Ravi is so uncomfortable with being called "Dr. Zacharias" that he asks his employees and event hosts not to refer to him by that title. The press release, which I have reproduced here as Appendix 4, cited "confusion" and a "difference in cultural norms" as one of the reasons people still refer to Ravi as "Dr. Zacharias." It assured us that "it is Ravi's custom to request for the inviting parties not to use "Dr." with his name in conjunction with any speaking events." But, they lamented, this is a matter that is sometimes "beyond our control."[101]

This was a most dishonest statement from Ravi's ministry. The paper trail shows Ravi aggressively referring to himself as a doctor all the way back to the early 1980's, and rarely disclosing that he was not. The only conceivable reason for him not *always* disclosing that his degrees were honorary is that he wanted people to think otherwise. The simple convention of putting "(Hon)" next to the doctorate unambiguously ensures that nobody will mistake an honorary degree for an academic one. But the way Ravi referred to himself during the past three and a half decades shows a clear intent to deceive.

Is this an unfair accusation against the evangelist? After all, while the practice of calling onself a doctor based merely on honorary degrees is gauche and misleading, it is a common one amongst evangelical Christian males.[102] Hasn't Ravi just been doing what Billy Graham did? Hasn't he merely participated in what RZIM calls "an appropriate and acceptable practice"?[103]

No. First, contrary to the spin attempts of his public relations team, the issue is not that he called himself "Dr. Zacharias" while only holding honorary degrees. The issue is concealment; Ravi routinely described his doctorates in a way that concealed their honorary nature. Second, thanks to Internet search services like the Wayback Machine we have access to a record that proves Ravi's deceptive intent beyond any doubt. Here is the smoking gun.

In November, 2016, after over a year of receiving complaints about his misleading credentials, Ravi added the word "honorary" to his official online RZIM bio. By December it was gone. In May, 2017, after more complaints,[104] it was added again. The same thing happened at Ravi's misleadingly-named "Oxford Center for Christian Apologetics."[105]

It is hard enough to think of a non-deceptive reason Ravi could have for not simply including the word "honorary" in his official bio. It is harder still to think of a non-deceptive reason why he would remove the word once it was there. Neither Ravi nor his P.R. team has even attempted to offer an explanation for these facts.

Ravi got away with misleading the public about the nature of his doctorates. This emboldened the ambitious evangelist to employ far more brazen tools of deception in the service of his public image. Ravi Zacharias soon began to boast about much bigger credentials that he never had. Let us go now to Cambridge, 1990.

CHAPTER 8: RAVI SPINS OUT OF CONTROL: THE CAMBRIDGE CLAIMS

"Imagine being in one of the most prestigious universities in the world, having the most prestigious philosophy department. I went there. I studied under them." - Ravi Zacharias on his studies at the University of Cambridge.[106]

The University of Cambridge has been a very big part of Ravi's self-presentation since 1990. He tells us that he was "educated in Cambridge"[107] and he routinely refers to various prominent Cambridge scholars as "my professor."[108] He makes frequent reference to having studied quantum physics at Cambridge under the renowned physicist Dr. John Polkinghorne to whom he refers as "my professor in quantum physics." In his memoirs he describes a bold confrontation he had with Cambridge philosopher Don Cuppitt, whom he describes as "my professor of philosophy."[109] Ravi also tells us that he was invited to be a "visiting scholar" at the University, and this claim appears widely on his book jackets and publicity materials.[110]

All of this is false. In August of 2018 Ravi admitted to the Christian psychology professor, Dr. Warren Throckmorton, what he had avoided admitting for years: he had never enrolled in classes at Cambridge.[111] Ravi had actually done a "guided study" at a relatively unknown Anglican training school called Ridley Hall for 2-3 months in 1990.[112] Ridley is in the town of Cambridge and has affiliations with the University through a theological federation of schools, but it is not and has never been a constituent part of the University of Cambridge.[113]

While at Ridley Hall Ravi sat in on lectures at the University. This single semester of observing classes at Cambridge while he was in his mid-40's is the sole basis for the "educated at Cambridge" claim that Ravi has loudly made for many years. It is also the sole basis for the impressive claim that he had been a "visiting scholar at Cambridge University."

We are fortunate that the evidence for this deception is all in writing and comes directly from Ravi himself and from the University of Cambridge. In his memoirs Ravi tells us this about his 1990 sabbatical in the town of Cambridge. "I spent part of that year at Cambridge University in England with my family, and it was a very special time for us. I was invited to be a visiting scholar, and I decided to focus my studies on the romantic writers and the moralist philosophers."[114]

I contacted Cambridge through their standard public information avenues and asked about Ravi's visiting scholar claim. They investigated and replied as follows: "We can confirm that Mr Zacharias spent a sabbatical at Ridley Hall where his supervisor was Dr Jeremy Begbie." In response to my follow-up they said "visitors at Ridley are not formally visiting scholars at the University of Cambridge." They also informed me that "[a]ttending lectures and classes at the University of Cambridge whilst on sabbatical at Ridley Hall would not confer University of Cambridge Visiting Scholar status on a student. Ridley Hall is not a constituent part of the University of Cambridge and has different criteria for granting Visiting Scholar status."

So Ravi had been on a sabbatical at the somewhat obscure theological school, Ridley Hall, and had converted it into a prestigious University of Cambridge "visiting scholar" position.

I presented this finding to Ravi's ministry. Their response provides yet another troubling example of how Ravi and his people prefer deception to confession. Please read closely. In mid-2015, upon learning that Cambridge had contradicted him, Ravi changed the "visiting scholar" claim at his website to reflect that his studies had been at Ridley Hall and not at the University of Cambridge. That is an accurate description. However, Ravi then falsely stated that when he was at Ridley Hall it had been more closely "affiliated" with the University. Here is what the statement from his ministry said: "Zacharias has been a visiting scholar at Ridley Hall, Cambridge (*then affiliated with Cambridge University, now more recently allied with Cambridge and affiliated with Durham University*) . . . ."[115]

So things were different in 1990. Ridley was more closely "affiliated" with the University of Cambridge back when Ravi was at the church training school.

It was a crafty move. Nobody would bother to check. But I did. Cambridge confirmed that there had been no changes in its relationship with Ridley Hall since 1990.[116] Ravi's talk of Ridley "then" being "affiliated" with the University and now being "allied" with it was sheer obfuscation. Ravi could not simply admit that he had been deceptive, so he deceived to cover it up.

Ravi's ploy failed, and after over three years of public criticism and pressure beginning in 2015 he eventually came clean. In April of 2018, he posted a new C.V. at his ministry website. His "visiting scholar at Cambridge" became a very modest, but accurately described, "guided study at Ridley Hall.[117] All references to being a "visiting scholar" anywhere vanished.

There was more. The University also informed me that the professor under whom Ravi so frequently claims to have studied quantum physics, Dr. John Polkinghorne, had not taught physics in 1990 at all. He taught two courses that year, one on Buddhism and one on the science/theology dialogue. In fact, by 1990, Dr. Polkinghorne had long since left the science faculty to become a priest. So Ravi audited a class on the science and theology dialogue and converted it into a claim, which he has made for decades, that he had studied quantum physics at Cambridge.[118]

The admission in August of 2018 that Ravi never enrolled at Cambridge also reveals that RZIM had misled the public in its defense of him. For after the Cambridge credentials were called into question his ministry released a statement in which they stated "all of Ravi Zacharias's courses were at the Cambridge University colleges and with University professors, under the supervision of Jeremy Begbie."[119] His ministry gave the public no hint that their leader had never enrolled in courses, that he had merely observed lectures. On the contrary, their statement suggests something much more formal and impressive.

So for about a quarter of a century Ravi Zacharias aggressively used a fabricated "visiting scholar" position in the service of his public image and claimed to have been educated at the University of Cambridge. Not a single Christian openly called him on it. When Ravi got caught he resorted to further deception to preserve his reputation.

It gets worse. Ravi had a Cambridge notch on his bedpost. Next he wanted Oxford. So he simply fabricated a professorship for himself at that great university. It was his boldest move to date. Let us take a look.

CHAPTER 9: RAVI'S GREATEST NON-SEXUAL LIE: "PROFESSOR AT OXFORD"

"Now I am a professor at Oxford." - Ravi Zacharias to an audience at the C.S. Lewis Institute on May 2, 2008.[120]

"I am not and have never been a professor at the University of Oxford." - Ravi Zacharias statement to Dr. Warren Throckmorton on 8/22/18.[121]

On May 2, 2008, Ravi Zacharias stood before a Christian audience at the C.S. Lewis Institute in Falls Church, VA, and told his biggest non-sexual lie. In the middle of a speech in which he lamented the lack of "leaders with integrity" Ravi told the audience "Now I am a professor at Oxford."[122]

Ravi has a long history of making impressive claims about his various positions at the prestigious University of Oxford. In his official bio from 2006 - 2008 he claimed to be "a Visiting Professor at Wycliffe Hall, Oxford University in Oxford, England."[123] (Wycliffe is one of the schools that constitute the University.) In his memoirs he called himself "an official lecturer at Oxford now, teaching there once a year."[124] In one television interview we see him tell his Christian interviewer that he lectures three times a year at Oxford, where, he informs us, Richard Dawkins also teaches.[125]

Despite his widespread boasts about Oxford, Ravi Zacharias has never held any position at the University. He knew his claims were false for he quickly removed all references to Oxford from his website bio after he learned that I was investigating his credentials in the summer of

2015.[126] I had not yet even mentioned Oxford, but he must have known it was coming.

By late 2015 I had become suspicious of all of Ravi's impressive academic claims. I contacted the University of Oxford to verify the claims about his various positions at their institution. The University informed me that it had no record of Ravi in its system and therefore that "we do not believe that he has ever been an employee of the University."[127] I also contacted Wycliffe Hall, a constituent part of the University where Ravi claims to have held the various teaching positions. Wycliffe informed me that "Ravi Zacharias has spoken at Wycliffe, but has never held any formal teaching position."[128]

So, despite many years of claiming the contrary, Ravi Zacharias has never held any position at Oxford. He has never been on the University's payroll and has never held a teaching position there. And while he heavily touted a "senior research fellow" position at the University, it turns out that this title was merely honorary.[129] And not only did he routinely fail to disclose that it was honorary, he often pretended otherwise. On February 13, 2013, Ravi went so far as to tell a fellow Christian apologist in an interview that his "senior research fellow" position at Oxford, which we now know was merely honorary, is "a credential with which I work in the academy" and when attending "an academic forum."[130]

After three years of searing criticism, on August 22, 2018, Ravi informed the Christian psychology professor and blogger, Dr. Warren Throckmorton, that he had never been a professor at Oxford. He made a tepid apology to Dr. Throckmorton (although nowhere else) about his prior Oxford and Cambridge claims. "I recognize that academic terms and designations are important, and I apologize for any occasion on which I have wrongly titled my association with either of these institutions."[131]

That Ravi actually thought he could get away with a falsehood such as claiming to be an Oxford professor speaks volumes of either the cynicism or the cowardice of his Christian colleagues in the God business.

As we saw, the Christian and Missionary Alliance seminary in Nyack, NY, let his false claims slide in the early 1980's. Ravi took the lesson to heart and built an international career on false credential claims, safe and secure from all alarm that a fellow Jesus follower might speak truth to power.

How was this famous preacher, the apostle to the academy, able to make such obviously false claims year after year in Christian academic circles with no repercussions? Where were the scholars at Ravi's autonomous Oxford Center for Christian Apologetics and those at Wycliffe Hall? Where were the Oxford scholars at Ravi's own ministry who knew so well that their leader was lying? Where was John Lennox? Or Os Guinness? Or Amy Orr-Ewing? Lennox is an Oxford professor, Guinness and Orr-Ewing both did doctorates at the University of Oxford. They knew full well that their leader was fabricating his credentials, yet they not only remained silent but continued to lend their names to Ravi's ministry and to accept speaking engagements in the name of that ministry. And where was the rest of the cast of devoted Ravi colleagues who have known for years about the bogus claims made by their leader in Christian ministry?

Let us now meet some of the people who have made Ravi's deceit possible. God may have the whole world in his hands. But the people we encounter in the next chapter hold in their hands something of far more immediate value; the flow of information to millions of Christian consumers.

CHAPTER 10: RAVI'S ENABLERS AT GOD, INC.

"But those elders who are sinning you are to reprove before everyone, so that the others may take warning." – 1 Tim 5:20

"One of the most godly men in the world." – Southern Evangelical Seminary spokesperson, Deborah Hamilton on Ravi Zacharias, 10/15/18.

"We inspire the world by meeting the needs of people with content that promotes biblical principles and honors Jesus Christ." - HarperCollins Christian Publishing Website.

In Hannah Arendt's *Banality of Evil* she speaks of those who are "terrifyingly normal." These are the "joiners," the decent people who just want to go about their business without being overly bothered by the big picture consequences of their actions, things like genocide or credential fraud. They contribute to injustice, but in a very innocent way. Most troubling of all, they consider themselves sincere, noble and devout as they do their enabling.

Could Ravi so widely claim to be a "professor at Oxford" when nearly everybody he worked with knew that it was false? Could he claim in his books and lectures to be a visiting scholar at Cambridge when everybody he worked with knew it was false? Could he claim to have studied quantum physics at Cambridge when his colleagues knew he had done no such thing?

Ravi Zacharias International Ministries

Alpharetta, GA
Founded: **1984**
Current Status: **Member**
Member Since: **April 1, 1986**
Click here to view the certified church's profile

Comparative Financial Data

	09/30/15	09/30/16	09/30/17
Revenue			
Cash Donations	$23,064,579	$42,707,749	$35,035,892
Noncash Donations	$4,173,388	$2,900,994	$2,817,768
Other Revenue	$1,260,132	$1,744,492	$1,186,798
Total Revenue	$28,498,099	$47,353,235	$39,040,458

The Evangelical Council for Financial Accountability shows Ravi's ministry generating tens of millions of dollars a year. Chart used with the kind permission of the ECFA.

Yes. It is an astonishing fact that during thirty five years of systematic credential fraud by the famous preacher not a single Christian had the courage publicly to speak out. It is not that they did not notice. As we saw earlier, theologian and apologist Dr. John Stackhouse told *Christianity Today* that evangelicals have "quietly mentioned" Ravi's exaggerated academic claims for decade. In a Facebook post he also said this: "I've been worried for 20 years about someone finally doing exactly this: calling Ravi Zacharias to account for inflating his academic credentials."[132] No Christian spoke out. Many decent Christians, however, enabled Ravi. Let us take a look.

Examples of "Joiner" Deception

Professor Jeremy Begbie

Jeremy Begbie provides a disturbing case study of the dynamic that made Ravi's deceptions possible. There is no scoundrel here, just an enabler who, I suspect, wanted only to get on with his work. Dr. Begbie was Ravi's supervisor at Ridley Hall. He was not a Cambridge professor at that time.

Dr. Begbie is a devout Christian, an accomplished musician, a fine scholar, and a professor who since his more humble Ridley Hall years has earned himself a position in the highest echelons of academia, Duke University. I have had several email exchanges with Dr. Begbie and I take him to be a decent human being and a man of integrity. But he enabled Ravi in perpetuating a false claim. Here is what happened.

Dr. Begbie supervised what Ravi now admits was merely a "guided study" in 1990 at Ridley Hall. As we saw, Ridley Hall is in the town of Cambridge but it has never been a part of the University of Cambridge. Dr. Begbie told me that Ravi's sabbatical at Ridley lasted for two to three months.[133]

As we have seen, Ravi misrepresented that guided study at Ridley as the more impressive "visiting scholar" position at Cambridge University. He also widely claimed in his speeches and published writings that in his time at Cambridge he studied "quantum physics" with the Cambridge physicist, John Polkinghorne. He refers to Dr. Polkinghorne as "my professor in quantum physics."[134]

When Ravi came under attack for having fabricated his Cambridge credentials Dr. Begbie was contacted for a statement of support. He confirmed, in writing, that Ravi had indeed taken quantum physics courses (plural!) with Dr. John Polkinghorne at the University of Cambridge. Here is Dr. Begbie's statement:

> I can confirm that Ravi Zacharias was a visiting scholar at Ridley Hall, Cambridge in 1990, under my supervision. His courses included guided research with Dr. Begbie, lectures from resident and visiting instructors in the Romantic writers, lectures at the University's Divinity School from Don Cuppitt, *additional courses in quantum physics with Dr. John Polkinghorne*, and studies in world religions with Dr. Julius Lipner and others.[135]

Ravi posted Begbie's statement at his website. In that same post-
ing Ravi's ministry stated that "all of Ravi Zacharias's courses were at the
Cambridge University colleges and with University professors, under the
supervision of Jeremy Begbie."[136]

It was a moment of well-deserved triumph for the evangelist
Quantum physics requires many years of high-level math. And the preacher
with only a B.A. in theology and a non-academic Masters in Divinity had
managed not just one course, but more than one in that brief sabbatical at
the Church of England theology school where he focused on the "Romantic
writers and the moralist philosophers."[137] During that sabbatical he also
wrote his first book, (which was not about physics), spent evenings stroll-
ing the campus with his family, acquired a border collie, and enjoyed the
"return to the idyllic days of our family's life."[138] That he managed to take
quantum physics courses in addition to all this was impressive indeed.

But the claim was false. The University informed me that Dr
Polkinghorne had not taught physics in 1990. He taught a class on
Buddhism and one on the science/religion dialogue.[139] Ravi could not
have not taken a quantum physics course (much less "courses") from Dr.
Polkinghorne. Although Ravi had failed to respond to multiple inquiries
about this, we now know that at the most he observed classes on Buddhism
and the science/religion dialogue.[140]

Dr. Begbie had misled the public in writing. But how could this be?
As a successful academician at a prominent university, on being asked to
vouch for the claims of a former student who was under suspicion would
Dr. Begbie not have taken care to independently confirm the claim he was
about to make to the public? Did he do so?

I asked Dr. Begbie about this. His reply: "Dr Zacharias spoke to me
of courses in quantum physics with Dr Polkinghorne....I have no particular reason to doubt his claim."[141]

Dr. Begbie had ample reasons to be suspicious of Ravi's quantum
physics claim. But when the evangelist was challenged he asked Dr. Begbie

for a statement of support for the improbable claim. Dr. Begbie offered his rubber stamp, no questions asked.

Dr. Richard Land, Southern Evangelical Seminary and The Christian Post.

Randal Rauser is a Canadian philosophy professor and Christian apologist. He is a frequent contributor to *The Christian Post* and has dozens of articles there to his credit. Each of his submissions to *The Post* has been published, except one. It was about Ravi Zacharias.

In September of 2018 Dr. Rauser interviewed me about my research on Ravi.[142]

He submitted the interview to *The Post* for publication. But they did not publish it. This was a first, and Dr. Rauser was given no explanation.

There is, it turns out, no mystery here. I soon learned that the executive director of *The Christian Post* is a certain Dr. Richard Land, who also happens to be the president of the Southern Evangelical Seminary (SES.) Dr. Land and the seminary have a long history of supporting Ravi. The seminary awarded Ravi its "Lifetime Achievement in Apologetics" award in 2016 and it had invited Ravi to speak at its apologetics conference scheduled for October 2018. Ravi was billed as one of the plenary speakers at the conference.

Prior to the conference Dr. Land issued a press release specifically welcoming Ravi to the event. He said "we consider Ravi, who has served as an SES adjunct professor and on the Board of Advisors, to be a vital part of the SES family."[143] Dr. Land also made himself available for interviews about the conference. But he did not respond to my request for an interview. In fact, two days after I contacted him and the rest of the SES faculty seeking comments about Ravi Dr. Land sent an email to his staff warning them that "there are many in secular and even faith-based media today who are trying to discredit Christian leaders and institutions." He offered no facts and gave no defense. He simply instructed his staff to refer all questions about the apologetics conference with Ravi as a plenary speaker to the seminary's P.R. firm.[144]

Did Dr. Richard Land kill the Ravi story? Was the embarrassment of a critical article about Ravi in *The Christian Post* one month before Dr. Land's apologetics conference too much for the seminary leader? Neither he nor his spokesperson, Deborah Hamilton, answered my questions about this. Ms. Hamilton, did, however, get back to me about other issues. And she did so with a troubling statement that reveals the depths of dishonesty, cowardice or naiveté that so often mark the evangelical response to evidence that one of their stars is a deceiver. I will share her reply in full.

Ms. Hamilton wrote the following a few days after I had spoken to her in some detail on the phone and after I emailed her, at her request, documentation of Ravi's credential fraud and suicide threat. Please note that in the *Christianity Today* article to which she refers Ravi said nothing about his Cambridge and Oxford claims, nor does he address his suicide threat. Oddly, this did not stop the seminary's spokesperson from making the following claims:

> Mr. Baughman, please see the article link below that directly explains the questions you had about Ravi Zacharias. This has satisfied many people who heard the rumors about one of the most powerful Christian apologists and one of the most godly men in the world, and has put questions to rest.

> Ravi Zacharias' heart is to lead people to an eternal relationship with our Lord and Savior, Jesus Christ. I have heard him speak in person and he is an incredible evangelist.

> Many have been so sidetracked by the enemy to take down this man of God, that they have wasted years of their lives on it. It is heartbreaking what satan has done.

What is really needed by those who don't know Christ is a transformed heart and mind that can only happen through the Holy Spirit. Ravi delivers messages that change the worldviews held by many but the enemy snatches the truth away from them. Jesus Christ loves people and offers freedom, joy, love, peace and a life above what anyone can ask or imagine if they give themselves completely to Him.

May God bless you.

https://www.christianitytoday.com/news/2017/december/ravi-zacharias-sexting-extortion-lawsuit-doctorate-bio-rzim.html [145]

This head-in-the-sand approach suggests that the leaders at the influential Southern Evangelical Seminary have little interest in learning about the serious misdeeds of Ravi Zacharias. The evidence is summarily dismissed as the work of "satan" (note lower case) and of those who have "wasted years of their lives" trying to bring down the man of God.

Equally troubling is the conflict of interest Dr. Land has in wearing a media hat and an activist hat simultaneously. Dr. Land and his seminary are heavily invested in Ravi Zacharias being an honorable man and have a strong incentive to suppress word of his misdeeds. As executive editor of *The Christian Post* Dr. Land is well situated to keep such news from his many readers. And that, it appears, is exactly what he did. Furthermore, the description of Ravi as "one of the most godly men in the world" also reveals the Orwellian extremes to which the seminary is willing to go to keep an influential member of the "SES family" looking clean.

Professor John Lennox

Another of the scholarly joiners who surrounds Ravi is the Oxford mathematician, John Lennox. Dr. Lennox is a regular speaker with Ravi's ministry and holds earned doctorates from both Cambridge and Oxford. Dr. Lennox is surely aware that Ravi does not have the math background to have taken quantum physics courses at the University of Cambridge where Lennox himself did both a Master's and Ph.D. But Dr. Lennox says nothing as Ravi speaks in his presence of quantum physics studies with Dr. Polkinghorne.

Dr. Lennox also knows of Ravi's false "professor at Oxford" claim.[146] As an Oxford professor himself one might expect him to be deeply troubled by the claim. But Dr. Lennox continues to lend his prominent name to Ravi's ministry.[147]

HarperCollins Christian Publishing

As of 2018, HarperCollins Christian Publishing (HCC) has published nine Ravi books either directly or through its subsidiaries. In June of 2017 I provided their assistant general counsel, Dan Foutz, with a substantial packet of documentation confirming extensive deceit by Ravi. In particular, I pointed out six false or significantly misleading credential claims Ravi had made in the memoirs that HCC had published through its subsidiary, Zondervan. That book is still in print. Mr. Foutz informed me that he would "dig into the background facts" and get back to me. Two weeks later he wrote, "We have no further comment Steve. Best wishes to you and have a great weekend."[148]

Five months later Ravi settled his lawsuit with Lori Anne Thompson on terms of secrecy that allowed him to avoid commenting on his suicide threat. I made sure Mr. Foutz was fully informed of these settlement terms and the evidence against Ravi. Mr. Foutz was presumably also aware that Ravi's post-settlement press release failed to address the most serious allegations. Four months later Mr. Foutz's company announced that it had signed a contract with Ravi for a new book, *Jesus Through Eastern Eyes*.[149]

The Christian and Missionary Alliance

Ravi's own denomination, the Christian and Missionary Alliance, tells us that it conducted a "thorough inquiry" of the sexting evidence. It announced in a public statement on May 5, 2018 that "the available evidence does not provide a basis for formal discipline under the C&MA policy." It reached the same finding regarding the credential fraud. The church gave no reasons for its findings, noting only that it is "not appropriate to publicly discuss the nuances of these allegations."

Here is the entire statement:

PUBLIC STATEMENT ON ACCUSATIONS AGAINST RAVI ZACHARIAS

Evidence does not provide basis for formal discipline under the C&MA policy.

Ravi Zacharias has maintained his licensing credentials through The Christian and Missionary Alliance (C&MA) for 45 years. Along with all C&MA licensed workers, he is subject to the Uniform Policy on Discipline, Restoration, and Appeal.

Recently Mr. Zacharias has been accused of exaggerating his academic credentials. Mr. Zacharias and his employer, Ravi Zacharias International Ministries, have revised and clarified their communications to address these concerns. The C&MA has determined that there is no basis for formal discipline regarding this matter.

Mr. Zacharias has also been accused of engaging in an immoral relationship with a woman through the use of electronic communications. The C&MA recently completed a thorough inquiry of these accusations, including interviews with those involved and a review of all available documentation and records. While it is not appropriate to publicly discuss the nuances of these allegations, the available evidence does not provide a basis for formal discipline under the C&MA policy.

Questions may be directed to Peter Burgo, at communications@cmalliance.org.[150]

The most striking feature of this public statement is that it tells us almost nothing. Did the church find that Ravi did *not* have an affair/threaten suicide/fabricate credentials? Or did it find that Ravi *did* do these things but that these things do not rise to a disciplinary level at the C&MA? Or did the church not feel it needed to even reach the factual questions because Ravi has now fixed whatever problems may or may not have existed? And if there was no formal discipline was there *informal* discipline? On so controversial a public issue as this we must presume that the C&MA carefully chose its words. And it is unlikely an oversight that their chosen words were devoid of content.

I followed up with Peter Burgo, the church's spokesperson for Ravi issues, and he had the following reply: "Because of privacy issues pertaining to credentialed workers, the C&MA is not able to publicly discuss the nuances of the allegations; nor is the C&MA able to substantiate the claims you assert below..."[151] He later informed me that "[t]hose who were involved in any disciplinary proceedings regarding Ravi have been highly committed to maintaining the confidentiality of those proceedings."[152]

This is odd, for there is no church rule requiring such secrecy. On the contrary the church's Uniform Policy on Discipline expressly allows the C&MA and its ecclesiastical authorities broad latitude "to disclose any information to outside parties" when it is "within their discretion." (C&MA Uniform Policy on Discipline, Restoration, and Appeal, [2018] section III[C])[153]

The C&MA is perfectly free to inform the public about its Ravi investigation. It simply chooses not to.[154] We may never know why. But we may assume that if the church had investigated and found the allegations to be false it would have said so in its press release. Instead it chose to say next to nothing.

Ligonier Ministries

The C&MA decision had far-reaching ripple effects. Take Ligonier Ministries, which was founded by the late R.C. Sproul, a respected scholar and a man who apparently led a scandal-free life. Ligonier has close ties to Ravi and in 2018, after the revelations about Ravi had surfaced, gave him a coveted speaking slot at its West Coast Conference on Defending the Faith.[155]

I contacted Ligonier and inquired as to their continued support of Ravi in light of the allegations against him. Here is their reply:

Mr. Baughman,

Thank you for taking the time to write us. Ligonier Ministries exists to serve the church of Jesus Christ, not to take the place of the church in fulfilling her appointed task of preaching the Word, administering the sacraments, and conducting church discipline. As such, it is Ligonier's policy to defer to the judgment of the visible church with respect to those teachers whom we choose to serve in various roles for the ministry. Since the visible church to which Ravi Zacharias belongs has determined that the evidence does not support formal discipline against him, and since he remains in good standing with his ecclesiastical body, Ligonier is pleased to continue our relationship with him at this time.

If you have any further comments or questions, please feel free to contact me.

Yours in Christ,
Steve

Steve Nugent
Resource Consultant
Ligonier Ministries[156]

The dynamic here is important. A prominent and respected apologetics group has made the Christian and Missionary Alliance the final arbiter of the guilt or innocence of the latter's most prominent member. Ligonier appears unbothered by this conflict of interest and the free hand it gives "the visible church" to protect its own. Ligonier appears to have merely washed its hands of any responsibility to look into the mounting evidence of misconduct by the famous speaker it hopes will continue to grace its conferences.

The Southern Baptist Convention / Dallas, June, 2018

On June 12, 2018, Ravi stood before a large gathering of Southern Baptists in Dallas. "Convictions," he told the crowd, will "drive you through life, especially in the toughest seasons of the soul."[157] Despite the mounting evidence of deceit and misconduct, the denomination had given him a prestigious speaker spot at the Southern Baptist Convention annual meeting.

Senior leaders in the SBC were well aware of the allegations against Ravi. Jim Lutzweiler, the Southern Baptist historian and archivist, had made sure of that.[158] The *Baptist Standard* had also heard the news. The *Standard* is a religious publication that "specialize[s] in news, features and opinion for Texas Baptists…"[159] According to their website, the publication's areas of coverage include the Southern Baptist Convention. Their managing editor, Ken Camp, told me that he had received queries about Ravi Zacharias and that he found the news about Ravi to be "intriguing and disturbing." Given that a renowned scandal-plagued evangelist was coming to Texas to address Baptists (about the importance of convictions, no less!) this seemed like a story that the publication would be eager to cover. It did not. Mr. Camp informed me that "it's just not a priority for us."[160] Ravi Zacharias was therefore able to stand before an auditorium of Southern Baptists and lecture them on convictions while the Baptist press and church leadership knew what he was hiding but said nothing.

This was not the first instance of high-level Southern Baptist complicity in the Ravi cover-up. Let us go now to Jacksonville, Florida, and watch Southern Baptist megachurch pastor Mac Brunson and his son, Pastor Trey Brunson, use the threat of physical force to keep unflattering news about Ravi from reaching their flock.

CHAPTER 11: THE PASTORS BRUNSON THREATEN FORCE IN DEFENSE OF RAVI

"Speak every man truth with his neighbor." – Ephesians 4:25.

B y January of 2018 it seemed hard to bestow an award on Ravi Zacharias without also giving Jesus the middle finger. The Southern Baptists in Jacksonville, Florida, decided to do both.

Mac Brunson was senior pastor at the First Baptist Church of Jacksonville, Florida, a megachurch founded in 1838. The church held an annual Pastors' Conference at which it conferred the Homer G. Lindsay Award for Lifetime Ministry on a worthy servant of Christ. Ravi was to be the 2018 closing speaker. The Conference theme was "How Shall We Then Pastor?"

The church had previously announced the Lindsay Award winner before the conference. This time they didn't. They won't say why. But the award was scheduled to be conferred immediately after Ravi closed the show, so it seemed likely that the man whose life's work stood marred by unrebutted evidence of systematic credential fraud, an online affair, and a suicide threat to cover it up was to be the new Lindsay Award recipient.

Mac Brunson knew all about Ravi. The Southern Baptist archivist, Jim Lutzweiler had seen to that. Several months before the Pastors' Conference he had sent a dozen or so emails to Brunson's church notifying them of the evidence of misconduct by their upcoming speaker.[161]

Jim had been a Ravi fan for years. He and his wife listened to Ravi's radio show every Sunday morning on their way to church. But Ravi's tendency to get facts wrong eventually made Jim suspicious. He investigated and soon became one of Ravi's most outspoken Christian critics.

Jim Lutzweiler (left, photo provided by Jim Lutzweiler), Baptist author and historian, was removed from a church Q & A by security guards at the direction of Pastor Trey Brunson (right, photo from Trey Brunson's Twitter account) when he wished to ask a question about Ravi Zacharias.

Jim was somewhat of an expert on church malfeasance. He was an award winning historian and had contributed eighteen chapters to the 2016 Broadman & Holman publication *Churchfails: 100 Blunders in Church History (and What We Can Learn from Them)*. He had also been a church archivist and keeper of the Paige Patterson papers.

Jim wanted to avoid having to document the 101st blunder of the church he loved and served.

When it became clear that Mac Brunson was going forward with the Ravi accolade Jim decided to take more assertive action. He would go to Jacksonville.[162]

The church had scheduled a public Q&A session for the last day of the conference. It billed that session as a "whosoever will may come" event. Jim assumed that included him.

The event was to be led by Pastor Brunson. Jim planned to stand up and very politely ask the pastor a difficult but fair question. And because Jim would be standing before hundreds, he wrote the question down beforehand.

> Br. Brunson. With the theme of this Conference being "How Should We then Pastor?", I am curious to know how you as a pastor handled the very difficult task of what to do about retaining Ravi as a speaker and a Homer Lindsay Award-winner in light of his romance, his suicide email, his demonstrably false and NDA-violating protestations of innocence to *Christianity Today*, and last but not least his false claims of having been a lecturer at Oxford and Cambridge Universities.[163]

Jim drove the 470 miles from Jamestown, NC, to Jacksonville the day before the event. And, speaking of blunders, that night in the church auditorium, through no fault of his own, he committed one that would derail his entire mission. While chatting with a conference attendee whom he did not recognize Jim expressed his concerns about Ravi and asked the young man what he knew about Ravi. The man did not seem to know much about the Ravi evidence, but he assured Jim that Lori Anne had a history of suing pastors. Then the two parted.

The Lord's ways may be strange and mysterious at times. But that night it was clear what He was up to, and that He was on Ravi's side. The young man turned out to be Mac Brunson's son, Trey. The next day the younger Brunson put his newly acquired intelligence into action for God's purpose of embargoing unflattering Ravi news.

The public gathering began promptly at 4:00 p.m. Jim stood to ask his question and before he could be handed the microphone Trey Brunson hurried over and said "No. Do not ask your question. If you do, I will call security."

As Jim later described it, "Out of respect for the fact that I was on someone else's property, I politely but still disgustedly complied with Trey's sort of ungodly mandate. His and Mac's invitation had been a bait-and-switch." Jim sat down and quietly observed the rest of the event.[164]

Trey wasn't done yet. When the Q&A was over Jim Lutzweiler, the long-time Southern Baptist, quietly made his way over to the auditorium where Ravi was scheduled to speak at six. Jim had no intention of asking a question, only to listen to Ravi and then to witness what he was sure would be an historic moment, a powerful Southern Baptist megachurch bestowing an award on an unrepentant deceiver, in the presence of fully-informed, smiling church luminaries.

Jim took a seat around 5:15 p.m. While seated he heard a security guard say that he was there to "make a scene." At 5:44 a security officer asked Jim to step out into the foyer where two "pistol-packing security guards who in size resembled retired middle linebackers of the JAX-Jaguars with the Chicago Bear, Dick Butkus, thrown in for lagniappe" escorted him from the building.

A bewildered Jim Lutzweiler walked to his car and began the seven hour drive back to Jamestown. And as he drove away the Jacksonville Southern Baptists proceeded to make history with their middle fingers.[165]

CHAPTER 12: RAVI SUES FOR SILENCE

"And if anyone wants to sue you and take your shirt, hand over your coat as well." - Matthew 5:40.

Despite the attempts of his able enablers, by the summer of 2017, Ravi Zacharias was a desperate man. Lori Anne had hired counsel and threatened to sue. It was imperative that Ravi beat her to the courthouse. If she got there first she would file documents such as emails, BlackBerry messages and a phone register showing that Ravi had engaged in conduct that would likely bring his empire down. So Ravi sued her first. His complaint was filed on July 31, 2017, and apparently in a hurry, for three days later his lawyers submitted an amended complaint to correct "typographical errors."[166]

It is an almost amusing side fact that just as he filed his lawsuit Ravi left the United States. And he did not merely leave; he went incommunicado for over a month. With his "file-and-flee" strategy, Ravi's August calendar went completely dark, a most unusual occurrence for the busy circuit-riding preacher.[167] Two weeks after filing his lawsuit Ravi blogged from an undisclosed location.[168] We then learned that he was on a dangerous mission that required great courage. He began his post with these words: "I can't say much 'til we are out of here." He informed us that he and his team were laboring for the Lord "in desert terrain, under torrid temperatures of about 115 to as high as 120 degrees." He told his followers "We need your prayers and God's protection as we serve in His will."

Lori Anne Thompson, 2005 photo by Laurie McVivar, *The Contact* September 23, 2005, at page 9, used with permission of *The Contact*.

It all sounded very adventurous, if not glamorous. But whatever courage Ravi summoned for that dangerous mission, it was not enough to get him to hold a press conference on the courthouse steps, announce his intention to clear his good name and to field questions from one and all about his alleged misconduct with a married woman. Ravi Zacharias chose instead to "serve in His will" by escaping. This cowardice, as we shall see, is apparent throughout his lawsuit. Ravi could, with His help, bravely enter ISIS territory, but he could not face Lori Anne Thompson, or his past.

It is hard not to chuckle further over a bit of irony that Ravi's P.R. team inadvertently treated us to around this secret adventure. Ravi's self-imposed exile, it will be recalled, was necessitated by the fact that he had crossed too many lines with a married woman. In what can only be seen as unfortunate P.R. planning, his first scheduled post-exile appearance was on September 9, in Bengaluru, India, where he was to deliver a lecture on "Living With Clear Boundaries."[169]

Back on track now. Ravi's lawyers came up with a very aggressive legal theory. They would allege that the Thompsons had carefully plotted an elaborate blackmail scheme involving levels of planning that only accomplished extortionists, and those who do not fear jail time, would consider undertaking.[170] Adopting this legal strategy was a desperate move by Ravi's high-powered Boston and Atlanta legal team. But, other than having their client come to Jesus, it was all they had. They drafted the complaint such that the costs of defense through trial in federal court would easily reach six figures for the Thompsons. Under such pressure the defendants would have a strong incentive to settle for less than the five million dollars their lawyer had requested.

Ravi's strategy was clever. His legal theory, however, was implausible even on its own facts. For it was Ravi himself, and by his own admission, who made the online sexual intimacy feasible by asking Lori Anne, a younger woman whom he hardly knew, to communicate with him via the "more secure" and encrypted BlackBerry.[171] It was Ravi who, by his own admission, continued to receive the sexual photos without notifying his board until legal action was imminent.[172] It was Ravi who claimed to have objected fiercely to the photos but who failed to offer a single item of evidence showing that he actually did so.[173] It was Ravi who loudly claimed to be a victim of a vicious defamatory plot, one that caused him "substantial harm,"[174] but who then dismissed his case on terms that forbid him from ever clearing his name. It was Ravi who publicly promised a vigorous defense against the outrageously false allegations but then quietly paid the Thompsons for their silence before they filed their evidence for the public to see.[175] It was Ravi who filed a document that presented evidence of his suicide threat, and who then inexplicably failed to address the allegation.[176]

It is especially inconvenient for Ravi Zacharias that he comes into this battle with serious credibility problems. A man who for so many years falsely claimed to be, among many other things, a professor at Oxford faces serious credibility obstacles when he offers an extravagant theory in defense of the reputation he systematically lied to preserve. The Thompsons enter this arena with no such baggage.

Ravi's biggest obstacle, however, is that his legal theory is extravagantly implausible, and that of his opponents is a very simple tale of a powerful religious man falling into sexual misconduct with a younger woman and then hiring reputation professionals to cover it up. Ravi's case flounders even more severely when we consider the evidence Lori Anne has to offer. We shall look at that evidence shortly, but first let us put the relationship between Ravi and Lori Anne in context.

As far as sex scandals go, the physical aspect of this one was mild. Ravi was never alone with Lori Anne. They lived 800 miles apart in different countries. The sexual conduct between them took place exclusively online and by telephone. Nonetheless, it was sexual. The evidence for that is strong, as we shall see. The same goes for the evidence that Ravi threatened suicide to cover up the affair.

As far as "he said / she said" stories go, we are fortunate that we hardly need to get into such a credibility contest. Even if we assume for the sake of discussion that the Thompsons are the sophisticated extortionists Ravi's lawyers have made them out to be, the preacher's lawyers and public relations advisors have disclosed enough to establish serious misconduct on the part of their client.[177]

For those who want to scrutinize my analysis in greater detail, I have provided Appendix 1, a detailed description of the sources I rely on in reaching my conclusions. If I were to fabricate or mislead it should be easy to catch me doing so.

Let us now remain open-minded and take a charitable look at Ravi's claims.

CHAPTER 13: RAVI SPEAKS

"He who begins by loving Christianity better than truth, will proceed by loving his own sect or church better than Christianity, and end in loving himself better than all." - Samuel Taylor Coleridge

Giving Ravi the Benefit of the Doubt

It is a common practice in both law and philosophy to evaluate your opponent's claim in a light favorable them. If his or her case fails even on a charitable viewing you may march to victory without the need for lengthy arguments over facts. In this chapter we shall take such a charitable view of Ravi's lawsuit against the Thompsons. We will assume that Lori Anne and Brad Thompson really were extortionists out to lure the famous preacher into a sexual situation that they could then use to blackmail him.

Here are the salient points in Ravi's federal complaint and press releases. Each of the following statements is significant, as will be clear when we form conclusions about the evidence. Please read carefully. "Plaintiff" refers to Ravi. "Defendants" refers to the Thompsons.

Ravi's Federal Complaint in Civil Action 17-cv-02885: The Straight Facts

On July 31, 2017, Ravi sued Lori Anne and Bradley Thompsons in federal court in Atlanta. The Thompsons, he alleged, had engaged in a conspiracy to "coax [him] into an inappropriate online relationship with Ms.

Thompson"[178] which they could then use to extort money from him. Ravi sued the Thompsons for conspiracy and racketeering, as well as for intentional infliction of emotional distress and invasion of privacy. Ravi claimed "mental suffering, emotional distress, and injury to his personal sensibilities and emotional repose."[179]

He sought "actual damages, statutory damages, treble damages, punitive damages, exemplary damages, attorney's fees, costs of litigation, special damages, general damages, and all other damages provided by Georgia law."[180]

The gravamen of Ravi's complaint is found in paragraph 21:

As part of the current scheme, Defendants decided that evidence depicting an inappropriate relationship (in person, online, or otherwise) between Ms. Thompson and a prominent, pious individual like Plaintiff would enable them to force the individual to pay an exorbitant sum of money under the threat of disclosure of such relationship to the individual's employer, wife, and the public.

Ravi met Lori Anne and her husband on October 3, 2014, after he spoke at a conference in Kingston, Ontario. The couple were "unusually furtive in their attempt to meet and maintain a conversation with plaintiff."[181] Lori Anne asked Ravi to "reach out" to her husband, who was interested "in learning more about RZIM and its mission."[182]

Sometime thereafter Ravi spoke at an event in Toronto. The Thompsons were there, as was Ravi's daughter. Lori Anne asked the daughter "intrusive questions about, among other things, Plaintiff's daughter's recent divorce." Ravi's daughter was "offended" by Lori Anne and found her "behavior and demeanor to be aggressive and disturbing."[183]

At some unspecified time, the Thompsons took Ravi and his wife, Margie, to dinner in or near Toronto. Margie told Ravi afterwards that she felt "uneasy" about the Thompsons.[184]

The Thompsons continued to be "relentless in their quest to get Plaintiff's attention and implant Ms. Thompson into his life. Ms. Thompson repeatedly contacted Plaintiff. As a result of Ms. Thompson's messages, Plaintiff began to consider Ms. Thompson as a friend, in addition to a fan and supporter of RZIM's mission and Plaintiff's work."[185]

In the early stage of communicating with Lori Anne, Ravi used "the email address [he] had used to contact her husband after first meeting them."[186] And although Ravi is a prominent lecturer who, "due to time constraints," is "unable to respond" to his many "fans and supporters,"[187] at some point he nevertheless "asked Ms. Thompson that she communicate with him via private BlackBerry Messenger . . . ." He did so because this would allow them to have "a more secure method of communication"[188] which he desired because he travels in dangerous countries where his phone can be hacked or taken.[189]

"Over the course of the two years following their initial meeting . . . Ms. Thompson attempted to escalate her relationship with Plaintiff."[190] She "gradually introduced inappropriate topics into conversations with [Ravi], and then eventually introduced sexual topics. For example, she began expressing her love for [Ravi], and then began making sexually suggestive statements."[191] At some point, she began sending him photos of herself partially clothed, and then nude.[192] Ravi repeatedly asked her to stop but she continued.[193] Ravi denies ever soliciting sexual photos.[194]

At some point Lori Anne agreed to stop sending the sexual material but then told Ravi that she could not help herself.[195]

Ravi attempted to block Lori Anne's continued unwanted communication but was unable to do so partly because she "created new BBM (Blackberry) identification numbers."[196]

At some point Lori Anne tried to visit Ravi in Georgia, but he "intentionally left the area to avoid contact" with her.[197]

In September or October of 2016 Ravi "cut off all contact with Ms. Thompson,"[198] but he "remained amicable out of fear for his family's safety and of potential damage to his professional reputation if he upset the Thompsons."[199]

On October 29, 2016, Lori Anne told Ravi that "she planned to tell her husband about the inappropriate messages she had sent [Ravi]."[200] She did tell Brad. Ravi then began communicating with Brad about what had happened. His last communication with Brad was an email on January 24, 2017, in which Ravi said, "Let me answer your question as best as I can without risk of seeming to avoid the full force of the responsibility. Whatever the reason the blame is real and inescapable." He later added, "By the way, with the determination to not continue what was wrong, I purposely never met her even once. When she paid a visit to Atlanta for other reasons, I deliberately was out of town."[201]

Ravi also alleged that "on at least one other occasion, the Thompsons have sought a sum of money from an individual whose employment related to espousing the Christian faith. Specifically, in 2008, Mr. Thompson filed a lawsuit in Canada against a pastor and a church, seeking damages based on allegations that the pastor used his religious position to coerce Mr. Thompson into making certain ill-advised loans and investments."[202] The Canadian case was dismissed in 2010 and "sometime after the settlement, the Thompsons began experiencing significant financial distress."[203]

Exhibit 1 to Ravi's Complaint

On April 26, 2017, Ravi received an "Extortion Letter" from Lori Anne's lawyer, Mark Bryant of Paducah, KY. Ravi's lawyers (inexplicably!) attached the letter as Exhibit 1 to their complaint, thereby making it a public record. I have included it as Appendix 3.

The letter indicated that Ravi's assistant had asked for Lori Anne's contact information at a Businessman's Luncheon in Ontario, where they first met. This began a "grooming process that lasted for months as you gained her trust as a spiritual guide, confidante, and notable Christian statesman." Lori Anne "was made to feel safe in the confines of a confidential relationship" and she "opened up" to Ravi about her life." Armed with that information and your excellent grooming skills, you chose to exploit her vulnerability to satisfy your own sexual desires. Not only did you engage in sexually explicit online conversations, but you also solicited and ultimately received many indecent photos of Lori Anne throughout the course of your communications with her."

The letter claimed that Ravi had threatened suicide to pressure Lori Anne not to tell her husband about their relationship. Mr. Bryant told Ravi he had a copy of the suicide email and a call register reflecting "many lengthy telephone conversations" between Ravi and Lori Anne. The letter demanded $5,000,000 "in the alternative of protracted and public litigation."

The letter also claims that the couple is in counseling, that Lori Anne is "medicated for post-traumatic stress and anxiety," that Brad attempted suicide after finding out about the affair and that their oldest child "has been devastated on so many levels and is struggling to make sense of it all."

Ravi's complaint focuses heavily on responding to the allegations in Exhibit 1, the "Extortion letter." In his complaint Ravi states that he "has never engaged in any of the misbehavior of the sort alleged in the Extortion Letter."[204] Upon receiving the letter he "immediately informed RZIM's Governance Committee" and retained counsel.[205]

In a written statement to MinistryWatch immediately after filing the lawsuit RZIM promised that Ravi would "vigorously defend himself against these harmful mistruths and extortion attempt."[206]

Notwithstanding that promise, on November 9, 2017, Ravi dismissed his lawsuit. He did so before the Thompsons filed an answer to the complaint. The federal court record shows that Ravi's lawyers allowed the Thompsons three delays of time to file their response.[207]

On December 3, 2017, Ravi issued a press release in which he denied all wrongdoing except having "been a willing participant in any extended communication with a woman not my wife."[208] He also stated the following:

"However, at this time, unfortunately I am legally prevented from answering or even discussing the questions and claims being made by some, other than to say that each side paid for their own legal expenses and no ministry funds were used."[209]

These are the claims made in the court by Ravi's legal team and to the press by Ravi himself. We will now see that these claims reveal two things. First, even his own presentation of the facts makes it likely that Ravi engaged in serious misconduct with Lori Anne Thompson. Second, Ravi allowed his lawyers to wage a demonstrably false and vicious public relations assault on the Thompsons, all to preserve the image he had cultivated since his youthful conversion to Christ.

CHAPTER 14: RAVI CONDEMNS HIMSELF

"Plaintiff asked Ms. Thompson that she communicate with him via private BlackBerry Messenger ("BBM") – a more secure method of communication than e-mail given its superior security and encryption capabilities."
– Paragraph 36 of Ravi Zacharias's Federal Complaint

R avi did not need the Thompsons to make the case against him. He does it himself in his own words and in those of his lawyers. Let us now look at the conduct that Ravi admitted to engaging in.

Ravi initiated the "more secure" encrypted communication with Lori Anne

The first red flag appears with Ravi's admission that, despite being a busy public figure who "due to time constraints" could not reply to "fans and supporters," he nevertheless asked Lori Anne, a woman he hardly knew and about whom both his wife and daughter felt uncomfortable, to communicate with him via his private "more secure" BlackBerry device. This cautionary measure was an essential step in Ravi and Lori Anne being able to have the "extended communication" that he admits they had. And it was Ravi, not the alleged extortionists, who initiated it. What was it about his relationship with this younger woman that made Ravi want an encrypted mode of communication?

Ravi failed to notify his Governance Council until he faced legal action

It appears that Ravi received sexual materials or intimate overtures from Lori Anne for a long time. By his own admission her attempt to escalate their relationship continued "over the course of the two years",[210] during which time Ravi tells us he diligently tried to block her messages. But Ravi said nothing to his ministry about this fatal attraction person who could do severe damage to his reputation and his empire. It took a legal threat to get him to inform his governance council. Ravi's response to this supposed long-term stalker is not one that we would expect from an innocent celebrity whose business success is so intimately dependent on his public image. It is, however, fully consistent with a man who was a willful participant in an extramarital affair.

Ravi failed to offer evidence that he objected to the nude photos

I invite each of you to put yourself in Ravi's place for a moment. You are a celebrity in a line of work where your reputation matters greatly. You are married man and have been faithful to your wife for 45 years. A married woman with whom you have only briefly been acquainted begins to send you nude photos of herself by BlackBerry. You in no way solicited these and you repeatedly ask her to stop sending them. This woman, however, "expresses her love" for you and tells you that she cannot help herself.

Under these circumstances, would you not immediately apprise your board of the situation? And, would you not make sure to put at least one cease-and-desist demand in writing so as to have a record of your objection to this inappropriate and potentially damaging conduct?

Assume that this person then accuses you of soliciting those photos and that you eventually have no choice but to wage litigation against her. Would you not make sure to include at least one copy of a cease-and-desist request in your lawsuit to show that you really were not a willing participant?

Ravi did none of this.

Ravi claims four times in his complaint that he pled with Lori Anne to cease her behavior.[211] But he offers no evidence that he did. We can be sure that Ravi would have included the following in his court filing if it existed:

"Lori Anne, I am truly shocked by the photo you sent me this evening. Please do not send me anything like that again. Please. Please. If you do I will have no choice but to notify my board and terminate all further contact with you."

But he didn't.

This omission is all the more revealing given that Ravi's Invasion of Privacy - Intrusion upon Seclusion claim requires him to make an affirmative showing that Lori Anne's conduct was unwanted.[212] Evidence of his objections to the nude photos would have fit not only naturally but necessarily with that legal claim. But he offered none.[213]

Ravi denies many things, but not the suicide threat

We must wonder why the Thompson's attorney claimed to have a copy of the suicide email if Ravi never sent one. One generally does not try to bluff someone who would obviously see through the bluff. And why would this attorney quote Ravi's precise "bid this world goodbye" language if Ravi had made no such threat? And why would Ravi fail to address the suicide threat in the complaint while he firmly denied other less serious accusations?

The Christian watchdog group, MinistryWatch, in its detailed investigative report about Ravi, had this to say about the suicide threat: "We doubt the absence of a rebuttal to this charge was an oversight by Zacharias or his lawyers and it suggests that the alleged extortionists do have some evidence to back at least this one claim up."[214]

Ravi's account is implausibly extravagant

Lori Anne's is simple. Here is Ravi's toughest sell: his extortion theory requires us to reach implausible conclusions not just about his own behavior but also about an astonishingly sophisticated blackmail scheme that the Thompsons launched. On Ravi's theory here is what the Thompsons must have planned for.

In Exhibit 1 we see that the Thompsons were in couples counseling after the affair ended, that Brad had attempted suicide, that Lori Anne was under medication, and that their oldest child was devastated by the affair.

The first three of these, if true, would generate documentation from professionals and possibly from the police. Those documents would be discoverable in court. The Thompsons would have been required by court order to produce their medical and therapy records and any police records relating to Brad's suicide attempt. If they could not, Mr. Bryant's letter would be exposed as a load of lies and the Thompson's extortion scheme would be finished, with them both potentially facing criminal charges and significant reputational damage. Their lawyer could have been subject to severe professional discipline if he had not bothered to investigate the Thompson's story prior making his claim against the evangelist.

Ravi's theory, therefore, requires us to believe either that the Thompsons didn't care about being exposed (and Mr. Bryant didn't either) or that they hired and fooled doctors and therapists (and maybe even fooled the police) in order to generate a written record that they could use in their extortion scheme.

Picture this: Lori Anne and Brad sitting in the therapist's office week after week putting on a show about how abusive Ravi Zacharias was, all for the sake of fooling the therapist into making notes that would later be useful in litigation.

And picture this: Brad faking a suicide attempt all for the sake of generating records that could be used down the road in court to show emotional damages.

71

Ravi's theory requires us to believe that this is exactly what the Thompsons did.

And what about that eldest child? The medical, psychological and school records of that child would likely have been subject to subpoena to see if the child had suffered emotional trauma due to an extramarital affair one of her parents had. This is one more layer the Thompsons would have had to prepare for in their elaborate extortion scheme.

More problematically for the extortionists, the oldest child was an adult when Mr. Bryant sent his letter to Ravi.[215] She would have been subject to deposition as a witness to the turmoil, or lack thereof, that Ravi had brought on her family. Did the Thompsons coach their daughter on how to perjure herself in the upcoming litigation?

There are still more puzzles in Ravi's version of the Thompson scheme. Ravi tells us that Lori Anne specifically wanted him to reach out to her husband. Why would *both* the Thompsons try to meet Ravi if the whole point was to simply get Lori Anne into his life and pants? Why would they take Ravi and his wife to dinner? And why would Lori Anne try to meet and get close to Ravi's daughter? These moves would seem only to complicate an extortion plot aimed simply at luring a prominent man with the sexual temptations of a younger woman. This conduct is far more consistent with the Thompson's claims than it is with Ravi's.

And why did the Thompsons not pick a target in Ontario, Canada, their local turf, where Lori Anne would have more opportunities for salacious rendezvouses?[216] Was a hugely busy traveling preacher who lived 800 miles away and infrequently passed through town really the best target for these sophisticated extortionists so desperate for money?

These are some of the questions that Ravi's claims against Brad and Lori Anne simply fail to address. By contrast, Lori Anne's claim only requires us to believe that a powerful elderly religious man initiated an online affair with a younger woman and then used his vast resources to cover it up.

Ravi admits wrongdoing

What are we to make of Ravi's confessions in paragraph 75? Recall that in this paragraph of his complaint Ravi made the following confessions in his email to Brad: "Let me answer your question as best as I can without risk of seeming to avoid the full force of the responsibility. Whatever the reason the blame is real and inescapable." Later in the same paragraph he said, "By the way, with the determination to not continue what was wrong, I purposely never met her even once. When she paid a visit to Atlanta for other reasons, I deliberately was out of town."

This oblique language raises several questions. For what exactly does Ravi accept blame that is "real and inescapable"? What was he up to that "was wrong"? Why was Ravi unable to simply tell Lori Anne that he could not meet her when she showed up in Atlanta? Why did he need to "deliberately" be out of town?

Perhaps we may chalk this up to Ravi simply having weak boundaries. Still, Ravi's conduct is surprising for a man whose only mistake was having "extended communication" with a woman not his wife. And it is exactly what we would expect of a famous preacher having an extramarital online affair.

Ravi gave up his right to clear his name

Finally, there is the puzzling fact that Ravi settled his lawsuit on terms that forbid him ever to offer evidence of his innocence. This is not the conduct we would expect of a wrongly accused man who cares so much for his public image. Again, MinistryWatch concludes: ". . . Zacharias settled the case before it went to trial where RZIM's assertions of the 'false claims' made against Zacharias could have been proven to indeed be false. One can reasonably conclude, therefore, the couple extorting Zacharias actually did indeed have damaging e-mails and texts from him."[217]

So let us regroup for a moment. This is where we find ourselves without even having heard from Lori Anne. On being wrongly accused of having an online affair and threatening suicide to cover it up, Ravi Zacharias did not do what an innocent person would do. He did not fight to clear his name, a name that the Good Lord presumably wanted him to keep as clean as possible for the sake of the Kingdom. Instead Ravi gave up his right to defend the reputation that his God-given mission depended on.

What about the rest of the evidence? Not surprisingly, it neatly confirms that Ravi Zacharias was sexually involved with Lori Anne online and on the telephone, that he threatened suicide to cover this conduct up, and that he lied publicly and in court about it. Let us take a look.

As we do, we must keep in mind how high the stakes are here for Ravi. If Ravi threatened suicide a lot more was going on than he has claimed. Indeed, if Ravi threatened suicide, he lied to the federal court, to the Christian media and to his followers and donors.

Here, now, is more evidence that this is exactly what he did.

CHAPTER 15: RAVI'S SUICIDE THREAT

"I have little doubt that the single greatest obstacle to the impact of the Gospel has not been its inability to provide answers, but the failure on the part of Christians to live it out." – Ravi Zacharias, May 14, 2018.[218]

R ecall that in the previous two chapters we took it as true that the Thompsons were extortionists. We saw that even if that were the case Ravi fell for it. His own court filings and press releases suggest misconduct on his part beyond the mere "appearance of impropriety" that he admitted to. Things look much worse for him when we look at the rest of the evidentiary record.

Ravi's suicide threat is shocking and extraordinarily damaging to his legal case, to his reputation, and to those who continue to support him while knowing full well what he did. It shows an internationally renowned Christian minister pressuring a married Christian woman, on pain of his own suicide, not to take a necessary step towards repairing her marriage. With the emails we are about to see, Ravi showed the world that his reputation was more important to him than the divine moral code he has so eloquently preached since his teenage conversion to Christ.

I urge you to read these emails carefully. A more complete email chain is at Appendix 2. If you doubt the authenticity of this email chain please note that Ravi quotes from it in his complaint.[219] The following four emails were sent the same day Lori Anne informed Ravi that she would confess their relationship to her husband that night.

From: Ravi <rakzach@gmail.com>
Date: October 29, 2016 at 4:38:00 PM EDT
To: Lori Anne Thompson <loriannethompson@*.*>
Subject: Re: Letter

Are you going to tell him it's me?

From: Ravi <rakzach@gmail.com>
Date: October 29, 2016 at 4:38:48 PM EDT
To: Lori Anne Thompson <loriannethompson@*.*>
Subject: Re: Letter

You promised you wouldn't Lori Anne. If. You betray me here I will have no option but to bid this world goodbye I promise

From: Ravi <rakzach@gmail.com>
Date: October 29, 2016 at 5:03:34 PM EDT
To: Lori Anne Thompson <loriannethompson@*.*>
Subject: Re: Letter

Can we not meet at lest once before you do this?
Please please

From: Ravi <rakzach@gmail.com>
Date: October 29, 2016 at 5:57:00 PM EDT
To: Lori Anne Thompson <loriannethompson@*.*>
Subject: Re: Letter

Little did I know that was the most dark and accursed day of my life. You will not hear from me again

Ravi has never denied making this suicide threat. This is especially significant given the fact that he has shown himself willing to deny other allegations against him. In his complaint he specifically denies soliciting the nude photos,[220] providing counseling to Lori Anne,[221] having a fiduciary relationship with Lori Anne,[222] sending her nude photos of himself,[223] having had inappropriate physical contact with Lori Anne,[224] etc. Despite the fact that the single most explosive allegation against him glares out from his own Exhibit 1, not once does he deny that he threatened suicide to keep Lori Anne from confessing to Brad.

It gets worse. Ravi has, in fact, privately admitted threatening suicide. In January of 2018, Jim Lutzweiler, the Southern Baptist historian we have met in previous chapters, informed me that he had just received an important email from a nationally known "senior minister" whose name he shared with me and whom I knew. This minister had asked Ravi about the suicide email. Ravi admitted to this minister that it was authentic. The minister told Jim, "He wrote it but contests . . . that it has been erroneously interpreted." (Ellipsis is provided by Jim.) Jim shared this information with me, but shortly thereafter received a request from the minister to keep his name confidential. Jim then asked me to do so. I agreed to.[225]

I suspect that Ravi has made a similar confession to other Christian leaders. Whether that is the case or not, it is uncontested that Ravi did indeed threaten suicide. And he has not denied it. This tells us that his relationship with Lori Anne was not the mere matter of the "extended communication with a woman other than my wife" that he claims was his only transgression. Ravi, it appears, has lied about a lot more than his credentials.

Let us now look at the rest of the evidence that confirms that Ravi's relationship with Lori Anne was both sexual and mutual.

CHAPTER 16: LORI ANNE SPEAKS

"If there is one serious criticism that can be made of evangelical or ortho-dox Protestantism, it is that it understands the theory of Christianity but not the practice." - Harold O. J. Brown, *The Protest of a Troubled Protestant* (1970)

The Julie Anne Smith evidence

After things fell apart with Ravi, Lori Anne was referred to an online advocate for clergy abuse survivors, a woman by the name of Julie Anne Smith. Ms. Smith is the founder of the Spiritual Sounding Board, which serves as a gathering place on the Internet for victims of clergy abuse.[226] The two had extensive email exchanges and phone conversations. Ms. Smith took notes of these conversations. Lori Anne also provided Ms. Smith with a lengthy To Whom It May Concern letter about Ravi and shared with her the suicide emails that Ravi had sent her.[227]

The communication between Lori Anne and Ms. Smith reveals that there was a sexually intimate online relationship between Lori Anne and Ravi. Unless Ms. Smith is lying and/or a very sloppy note-taker, we may con-sider her statements to be almost as good as a first-hand account from Lori Anne herself. Lori Anne, of course, could have lied to Ms. Smith in hopes of building a record for her future litigation. That would have involved con-siderable fore-planning given that she began speaking to Ms. Smith around August of 2016, a full eight months before she threatened litigation.

It is not out of the question for a sophisticated extortionist to think that far ahead. But it seems more probable that Ravi just did what powerful preachers often do, and that his victim sought help. In the course of getting that help she revealed to her support persons what Ravi had done to her.

Julie Anne Smith made the following public statements in which she shared information that she had received from Lori Anne.

On November 24. 2017 Ms. Smith tweeted the following:

> I have seen correspondence between Ravi Zacharias and Lori Anne Thompson. He most certainly was an active participant in this online sexual relationship. He just has the $$ and was able to get this hushed via settlement.[228]

On December 4, 2017, Ms. Smith tweeted the following:

> This was not just about her sending nude pics. According to the victim, he requested the nude pics. This was online sex. He was an active participant. He complimented her. This was his initiative. This info is from victim's 20-pg narrative she sent me long b4 lawsuit.[229]

That same day Ms. Smith also tweeted:

> Absolutely: the PhD issue is small compared to grooming a vulnerable woman and eventually having phone sex (per victim's note that she sent to me).[230]

Two days later at the request of a *Christianity Today* reporter, Kate Shellnut, Ms. Smith provided the magazine with a written statement that included the following:

> The defendant told me that Mr. Zacharias initiated the idea of sending nude photos. He not only initiated in asking for nude photographs, but he was also specific in the types of images he wanted to see (specific sexual body parts.) I believe this is the reason why Mr. Zacharias wanted to settle this lawsuit. He certainly would not have wanted this information to come public in the discovery process of this Federal lawsuit.[231]

Anyone choosing to disbelieve these statements must conclude either that Ms. Smith fabricated them or that Lori Anne did so. This theory is implausible compared to the straightforward "dog bites man" account of a powerful man taking advantage of a weaker woman. Lori Anne's story is also free from the puzzles that Ravi's raises. And she comes to this dispute unhampered by thirty-five years of deceptive practices.

Lori Anne's blog

There is another fact that weighs very heavily against Ravi's extortion plot theory. Because of the NDA Lori Anne cannot legally speak about Ravi. But she can speak about clergy abuse in general. And she does so, eloquently and with a palpable passion, at her blog, where she advocates on behalf of victims of sexual violence by clergy.[232] Lori Anne has also begun graduate school to take an "MA in Child Advocacy & Policy." She says "My specific goal is first to study, then to educate and widely communicate on, the anatomy of sexual abuse in a faith-based community."[233]

I challenge any Ravi defender to spend ten minutes reading Lori Anne's essays and conclude that she is an insincere or dishonest individual. Someone in "severe financial distress" who conspires successfully with her husband to blackmail a celebrity preacher on bogus clergy abuse allegations and who gets her money from the unfortunate clergyman does not usually thereafter throw herself into advocating for survivors of clergy abuse.

It could happen, of course. But what motive would Lori Anne have for pretending to care about clergy abuse after she had successfully extorted money from Ravi? The more likely scenario is that Lori Anne genuinely cares about clergy sexual abuse. And if she cares about that issue I take it to be extremely unlikely that she would falsely accuse a man of clergy abuse just because she and her husband needed the money. But that is exactly what Ravi's theory requires us to believe.

Lori Anne gets mad (in a Canadian sort of way)

Recall that Ravi had a team of Boston and Atlanta lawyers on his side. He knew he could push Lori Anne around in the post-settlement phase. She had just gone through a gut-wrenching legal episode that had finally reached a resolution.[234] She and her family could now move on. Ravi knew she would be unlikely to risk landing back in court by fighting him at this post-settlement stage. He had a relatively free hand. And he used it.

On December 3, 2017, Ravi Zacharias showed the world what a bully he was. With the NDA in full force and effect, and Lori Anne legally bound to silence, Ravi issued an 813 word press release in which he accused her of "shockingly" sending him "extremely inappropriate pictures" that were "unsolicited." He claimed that he "clearly instructed" her to "stop contacting me in any form" and that "I blocked her messages, and I resolved to terminate all contact with her." (Recall that these were the very claims Ravi failed to produce a shred of evidence for when the lawsuit was underway.) In essence, Ravi called Lori Anne a promiscuous liar when he knew she could not reply. (For Ravi's entire statement see Appendix 5.)

On that same day Ravi showed the world the coward in him when he refused to answer questions about his suicide threat on the grounds that the NDA prevented him from discussing the case. "Zacharias," said *Christianity Today*, "declined to comment to *CT* on the image of the emails showing the apparent suicide threat, citing the non-disclosure agreement."[235]

This was a brazen violation of the settlement agreement. I contacted Lori Anne and suggested that she take legal action against Ravi. Her response is telling. To my surprise this person who had been so quietly resolved to Ravi getting his way with the public spin not only expressed an interest in my proposal but she told me later that she had consulted an attorney about the matter.[236] Her interest in pursuing legal options against Ravi was not what one would expect of someone who has just successfully pulled of an extortion scam. By then Lori Anne had her money, or at least the first portion of it. If she were a happy blackmailer it is unlikely that she would ponder further legal action against Ravi or even bother conducting an email discussion with someone like me who was seeking information about the lawsuit.

Lori Anne's conduct is fully consistent with a woman who was outraged at the prominent minister who had just agreed to mutual silence and was now publicly hurling false accusations at her. But Ravi got lucky. Lori Anne decided against suing him for breach of their non-disclosure agreement.

Let us take pause for a moment. At this point in our evaluation of the evidence everything seems to be working against the preacher. All evidence points to a man who used the gospel to give himself a sense of worth, who then used fabricated credentials to make himself a star on the preaching circuit, and who then got into a sexting situation that required a fancy legal team to suppress. There is one item of evidence that may work, however minimally, in his favor.

Ravi, it may be recalled, alleges in his complaint that Brad Thompson had previously sued a pastor and that sometime after the case was settled the Thompsons "began experiencing significant financial distress." If true this would provide a motive for their extortion plot. As trial lawyers know, having a motive does not mean that the person followed through with the alleged conduct. But it is a start. And since it may be the only thing that Ravi has going for him let us take a close look at his claim. (Spoiler alert! Ravi's "significant financial distress" claim turns out to be bogus.)

CHAPTER 17: LORI ANNE'S NON-EXISTENT FINANCIAL DISTRESS AND LITIGIOUS HISTORY

The couple with a litigious history.

Ravi correctly states in his complaint that in 2008 Brad Thompson "filed a lawsuit against a pastor and a church, seeking damages based on allegations that the pastor used his religious position to coerce Mr. Thompson into making certain ill-advised loans and investments." That case was filed in Canada and was dismissed in 2010.

Ravi's complaint incorrectly states that "the Thompsons have sought a sum of money from an individual whose employment related to espousing the Christian faith." Lori Anne was in fact not a party to that lawsuit.[237]

As experienced litigators, Ravi's lawyers knew that evidence of a prior litigation history is, with very narrow exceptions, not admissible in the federal courts.[238] But they made the allegations about the prior lawsuit anyway. This tells us that they were not above drafting their legal documents in a way that served the public relations interests of their celebrity client, even if it meant stretching the rules a bit.

Ravi's lawyers also knew, or should have known, that the particular facts of Brad Thompson's Canadian lawsuit made it a near certainty that it would not be admissible in Ravi's lawsuit. Brad's lawsuit really was legitimate and the pastor he sued was subsequently disciplined and suspended by his church for, among other things, doing precisely the sorts of things Brad said he had done. The church synod found that the pastor had "abused his office for inappropriate ends and/or self-interest by soliciting and/or allowing a counselee and her husband, both of whom were parishioners, to invest in companies that he and his family owned."[239] In May of 2013 the church issued a confidential "Safe Church Advisory Panel Process Report" that found that this pastor had committed dozens of acts of misconduct with dozens of complaining parishioners.[240] But Ravi's legal team mentioned Brad's lawsuit in the complaint anyway, knowing that Ravi's supporters would read it as favoring the extortion plot theory.[241]

It wasn't honest, but it was a smart public relations move. The Christian press repeated the story of "the couple" having filed a prior lawsuit,[242] and the false allegation lit up the base: "This wasn't the first time these two tried to extort money."[243] Even the generally fair minded MinistryWatch referred in its investigative report to the "couple with a litigious history seeking a $5 million extortion payment from [Ravi]."[244]

The truth is that "the couple" never filed a lawsuit, and Brad's lawsuit had nothing to do with extortion. It was a legitimate complaint against an unethical pastor. But Ravi won that battle on the public relations front.[245]

Significant financial distress.

In another dirty trick, Ravi then alleges "on information and belief" that sometime after the dismissal of the Canadian case in 2010 the Thompsons "began experiencing significant financial distress." If this were true it would be a fair claim to make, for if the Thompsons were desperate for money they were more likely to resort to criminal means, such as extortion and blackmail, to acquire it. And if the Thompsons were desperate for money in 2010 they might also have been so in 2014, when they met Ravi. And if they were desperate for money in 2014 they might have been more likely to form a complex plan to extort money from some famous person.

So they alleged in the complaint that Lori Anne and her husband were in tough financial straits.

Was the claim true? Notice that when Ravi's lawyers alleged that the Thompsons fell into "significant financial distress" they did so "on information and belief." This is lawyer speak for not having personal knowledge of the truth of a claim but representing to the court that you believe it anyway. Lawyers make allegations "on information and belief" all the time. There is nothing improper about it. But it is not a license to put anything you wish into a document being filed in a court of law. In fact, Rule 11(b) of the Federal Rules of Civil Procedure requires that lawyers make allegations in court papers only if their beliefs about the truth of these allegations are "formed after an inquiry reasonable under the circumstances."

Did Ravi's lawyers do a reasonable inquiry into their claim that after 2010 the Thompsons fell into a state of "significant financial distress"? It doesn't look like it. But I did.

I hired a private investigator in Ontario who looked into the Thompsons financial situation from 2010 to 2018. Here is what he reported: "We have undertaken a due diligence investigation and research with available records regarding the financial abilities of the Thompsons between 2010 and the present and can find no indications of any monetary hardship."[246]

Had Ravi and his legal team fabricated the claim to make their blackmail theory more viable? They won't say.[247] But it sure looks like it.

CHAPTER 18: THIRTY PIECES OF SILVER: THE NON-DISCLOSURE AGREEMENT

"Due to the settlement, which one can only presume was achieved by Zacharias personally paying the alleged extortionists some sum of money, it now appears clear he was likely guilty of something in this situation which would cause him significant reputational damage..." - MinistryWatch Report at Appendix 6.

As we have seen, Ravi was in a tight spot. A woman with whom he, at the very least, had crossed significant boundaries was about to sue him. Such urgent matters are generally too important to be left to quaint practices like prayer or trust in God. Ravi needed a real-world Comforter, a lawyer willing to throw in as many causes of action as s/he could think of and put extreme psychological and financial stress on the Thompsons. A federal lawsuit from first filing through trial can easily run into the hundreds of thousands of dollars in attorney fees, investigative costs, and miscellaneous fees. If the Thompsons wanted to prove what was on that phone that Ravi admitted he was about to destroy,[248] the forensic recovery costs alone could be in the tens of thousands of dollars.[249] So Ravi sued.

Ravi's lawsuit was a classic pressure move designed to bring the couple from Belleville, Ontario, to the negotiating table with a reduced money demand. It worked. The Thompsons lowered their demand to something Ravi would pay, and the case was settled on November 9, 2017.

MinistryWatch concluded that Ravi paid the Thompsons. There was ample evidence for this. The watchdog group noted that Ravi's ministry had been non-responsive to a question about payment: "While RZIM has stated to us the ministry made no payments in the settlement of the case (presumably any payments made to the alleged extortionists came directly from Ravi Zacharias), they did not answer our question if Zacharias has received any unusual compensation from the ministry recently which may have assisted him in making payments to settle the case."[250] So Ravi's ministry willingly disclosed that it had paid nothing to settle the lawsuit, but evaded the question about whether it had reimbursed Ravi for payments that he had personally made.

Further evidence of payment comes from the fact that the Thompsons made significant lifestyle changes after the settlement. In February (three months after the settlement) the family took a vacation trip to St. Lucia in the Caribbean.[251] By the summer of 2018 they had moved to a new city and Lori Anne had left her job and begun a graduate school program.[252] This is not conclusive of newly acquired wealth, but it sure smells of it.

The terms of the settlement are strictly confidential under the non-disclosure agreement (NDA). But we know two things. First, Ravi, as we saw, would pay Lori Anne for her silence. Second, both parties are forever prohibited from speaking about the case.[253]

Ravi references the agreement in his December 3, 2017 press release in which he stated the following: "All communication with both of them has concluded, and the legal matters have been resolved. However, at this time, unfortunately, I am legally prevented from answering or even discussing the questions and claims being made by some, other than to say that each side paid for their own legal expenses and no ministry funds were used."[254]

What is most astonishing about this press release from Ravi is that in the same document in which he claims that he cannot discuss the allegations against him he accuses Lori Anne of a wide range of shocking conduct. In the press release Ravi also says: "In my 45 years of marriage to Margie, I have never engaged in any inappropriate behavior of any kind."

His only error, he tells us, was to become "a willing participant in any extended communication with a woman not my wife." [255]

Christianity Today included Ravi's entire press release (and the one about his credentials) in its December 3rd article about his troubles. It is concerning that neither of the two reporters for the magazine, Kate Shellnutt and Sarah Eekhoff Zylstra, offer their readers any indication that they noticed his selective and convenient invocation of the NDA. When asked about his suicide threat Ravi said he could not talk. Then he talked about what he wanted to talk about. And the influential Christian magazine let it slide.

The failure of *Christianity Today* to comment on this is especially troubling since the suicide emails that Ravi claims he cannot discuss severely undermine the very denials he made in the same press release that *CT* reprinted in its article. In the emails that Ravi has never disavowed he not only threatened to take his life but he begged Lori Anne to meet him to talk. This picture is sharply at odds with the one in his court complaint and press release that portray a man of God diligently resisting the advances of a determined and promiscuous woman with blackmail on her mind. It also contradicts Ravi's claim that his only failing involved an appearance of impropriety by having "extended communications" with a woman not his wife.

The Thompsons request mediation.

There is one other improper disclosure that Ravi made on December 3 that we should discuss. It offers further insight into the cynicism behind Ravi's legal strategy and his willingness to manipulate his supporters and mislead the public.

In his press release he says, "The other side requested mediation rather than going to trial."[256] Discussing the process by which a settlement was reached is likely a violation of a non-disclosure agreement. But Ravi did it because he knows that the public at large, and especially those who form his base, are legally unsophisticated and will view the Thompson's request for mediation as a sign of weakness.

But all lawyers know that requesting mediation says nothing about the strength of one's case. In fact, the requesting party often is the one with the "slam dunk" case, the party who knows that their opponent will pay up quickly. Why bother with the trouble of a trial when you can obtain justice cheaply and quickly from your desperately wrong opponent?[257]

And that is exactly what happened. The Thompsons requested mediation, and Ravi paid up.

Ravi's eagerness to settle the case is also clear from his behind-the-scenes maneuvering. His side granted the Thompsons three extensions of the deadline for them to put their response into the public record, and then settled the case shortly before that response was due.[258] The federal court record shows that Ravi did not want the Thompsons to make their documentation public.

The evidence is clear; Ravi not only violated the NDA with his December 3, 2017, press release, but did so in a way that was misleading, evasive and cowardly.

Meanwhile the Thompsons have steadfastly and honorably refused to discuss what happened between them and Ravi. When I asked Lori Anne questions about Ravi and the case she firmly told me, "I can't say a bloody thing."[259]

CHAPTER 19: REMEMBERING
OUR HUMANITY

"I am always in your debt as a gift from God. What happened then will never happen again." Ravi Zacharias email to Brad Thompson on 12/5/16. (Appendix 2.)

Ravi Zacharias has publicly called Lori Anne Thompson an extortionist. If she was, Ravi cannot be faulted for describing her as such in defense of his reputation and his life's work. If she was not, Ravi's lawsuit and public statements about her constitute an act of great treachery that should disqualify him from any position of trust.

As we have seen, the evidence is so strongly against Ravi that even his staunchest supporters, including his own ministry, have chosen not to attempt a serious refutation. And Ravi, for his part, won't talk.[260]

Now, this is not to say that all is pretty on the Thompson front. Mark Bryant's $5,000,000 demand letter looks exactly like what we all think an act of blackmail looks like: "$5 million dollars" payable within thirty days "in the alternative of protracted and public litigation." Did Mr. Bryant actually get the Thompson's consent prior to sending the $5,000,000 demand? Lawyers do sometimes unilaterally put out a large figure in order to get a negotiating process going. We do not know what happened in this case. All we know is that it was indelicate lawyering and it provided public relations ammunition against the Thompsons.

More substantively, I am deeply disappointed that the Thompsons settled this case. Of course, it was clear at the outset that it would happen.

Ravi needed to make his sex scandal disappear from public discussion as quickly as possible and he had the money to make that happen. The Thompsons had the evidence that would make Ravi pay. Ravi took the initiative, came up with a legal theory that would have cost the Thompsons dearly to defend against. Lawyers do not take defense cases on a contingency fee because 40% of "Final Verdict: Ravi Zacharias is an incorrigible liar" is zero.

Things played out as Ravi planned. He offered the Thompsons a handsome payout in exchange for a vow of silence. They took the deal, and then the family vacation.

The settlement is unfortunate because Lori Anne had in her possession conclusive evidence that would have served a tremendously worthy cause. Clergy sexual misconduct has forever been a scourge on religious life. The Thompsons had a spotlight to shine on the methods and machinations of one of the most influential evangelists in America.

Might there be other women out there who would have found healing and courage in seeing Lori Anne fight back? At age 68 was this really Ravi's first act of extramarital bullying and deception? Even if it was, it had much to teach us about the grooming process used in clergy sexual misconduct cases. But the Thompsons let Ravi buy their silence for what must have been a handsome sum.

My disappointment, of course, does not justify me in judging the Thompsons too harshly. We do not know what went on behind the scenes. What threats did Ravi and his lawyers make? What, indeed, are Ravi and his defenders capable of? Vested interests abound. A multimillion dollar industry rests on the name of this one man. Are there among its beneficiaries people capable of drastic, illegal and violent action to preserve the benefits that flow from Ravi's success? Despite my own insignificance to Ravi's empire a threat was made to me the morning after I told Ravi I had his suicide email in my possession. What more might the Thompsons have faced?

Furthermore, if Ravi had betrayed Lori Anne with his nasty lawsuit, as seems almost certain, it would be hard to blame Lori Anne for just wanting the whole episode to be over. In a September 2018 blog post Lori Anne quotes from an article on NDAs by a certain Dr. Scott McKnight:

> Fact: By the time victims get to the NDA stage, usually they have been dragged through hell and back. The legal process presents a veritable traumatic merry-go-round, complete with evil clowns and financial loss through limitless legal costs. Add in the well-played instrument of fear, this is nothing short of disorienting, if not despairing for victims of clergy malfeasance (sex, money or spiritual abuse).

> The Demandee has already been overwhelmed by the Demander . . . the power dynamic did not ever change. The victim is often coerced, if not with words, then with the overwhelming reality that the balance of power was and remains in the hands of the powerful offender.[261]

More importantly, there are times when an agenda, even a worthy one, should take a back seat to a victim's need to heal. Here are Lori Anne's own words:

> The plumb line in recovery from sexual violence is the restoration of power and control to the victim. Priority number one is her safety: physically, emotionally, psychologically, relationally, and spiritually; NOT any other agenda; however well intended.

> To be blunt… it is NOT the victim's responsibility (moral, ethical, spiritual, legal, civil etc.) to expose the perpetrator and lead the way for corrective action. To coercively coax a victim to speak, or speak on her behalf without her expressed permission is to disempower her again.[262]

If we can agree on nothing else, let us agree that there really are powerful religious men who abuse women (and men) and then lie about it, causing their victim to suffer guilt, loss of self-esteem, intense loneliness, and a sense of confusion that disorients and makes it hard to find a direction home. And there really are powerful religious leaders in the God Business who support their abusive Christian colleagues in covering it all up.

When a situation presents as even possibly one of abuse, the wise observer's first priority, in an ideal world, will not be to defend the Ravi, but to ensure that there is not a victim who needs support here and now. Only after we are sure that there is no victim, merely a lying opportunist or an extortionist, should we return to defending or excusing the Ravi. Sadly, very sadly, that is a view that has never gained much currency in this land, the United States of America, that so strongly prefers indignation to wisdom.

Ravi made mistakes. Ravi crossed boundaries. Ravi exaggerated. And for decades Ravi just plain lied. But Ravi Zacharias's greatest act of indecency has been to demonize Lori Anne Thompson for the sole purpose of preserving his public image. Fortunately for Ravi his Christian business colleagues have conveniently interpreted the Lord's command to turn the other cheek as permission to turn the other way.

APPENDIX 1: MY SOURCES

Here are the evidentiary sources on which I base my conclusion that Ravi Zacharias had an extramarital online affair, threatened suicide to cover it up and then lied in federal court and in his December 3 press release. I present them in rough order of significance.

1. Ravi's federal Complaint filed in Atlanta on July 31, 2017. This is a legal document in which Ravi states his claims against the Thompsons and outlines his relationship with them from beginning to the onset of litigation. Exhibit 1 to the Complaint (which I have reproduced here as Appendix 3) is a legal demand letter from Ms. Thompson's lawyer that describes Ravi's conduct towards his client as sexually exploitative. In the letter Mr. Bryant claims to have a copy of Ravi's written suicide threat. The letter also presents a demand of US$5,000,000 to avoid "public litigation." Significantly, in his Complaint Ravi denies many of the particular allegations Ms. Thompson made in that letter but he does not specifically deny threatening suicide in order to pressure her not to tell her husband about the affair. He also admits receiving nude and sexual photos from Ms. Thompson and not telling his Governance Council about these until she threatened litigation. In paragraph 75 Ravi cites a January 24, 2017, email to Brad Thompson in which Ravi seems to admit wrongdoing: "Let me answer your question as best as I can without risk of seeming to avoid the full force of the responsibility. Whatever the reason the blame is real and inescapable." He later adds, "By the way, with the determination not to continue what was wrong, I

purposely never met her even once. When she paid a visit to Atlanta for other reasons, I was deliberately out of town . . . ." (Ellipsis in original)

2. The email exchanges between Ravi and the Thompsons. These include his suicide threat and his plea to meet Lori Anne before she told Brad. These emails were provided to me by Julie Anne Smith, a Christian blogger and advocate for clergy abuse victims. Ms. Smith received these directly from Lori Anne. Ravi has never denied their authenticity. While some Ravi defenders have speculated without any evidence that the emails are forgeries, Ravi himself has never done so, and he quotes from two of them in his complaint. These are reproduced as Appendix 2.

3. Ravi's December 3, 2017, press release in which he criticized Ms. Thompson in detail and denies all wrongdoing except that involving an appearance of impropriety. Ravi specifically denied soliciting the erotic photos, but did not deny the suicide threat. This is reproduced as Appendix 5. Ravi's press release of the same day responding to the credential fraud allegations is at Appendix 4.

4. Portions of Ms. Thompson's "To Whom It May Concern" statement which she provided to Julie Anne Smith as well as Ms. Smith's notes from her lengthy phone calls with Ms. Thompson. I have not seen either of these, but Ms. Smith has shared some of the contents publicly and with the Christian media. These are important as a record of Ms. Thompson's claim that she and Ravi engaged in phone sex.

5. The Christian watchdog group MinistryWatch released a thorough report of its investigation into the Ravi allegations. Most of this is an analysis of evidence and is not itself evidence. But the report does provide evidence that Ravi paid the Thompsons for their silence and that he may have been reimbursed by his ministry. The entire report has been reproduced as Appendix 6, with the kind permission of MinistryWatch.

APPENDIX 2: EMAIL EXCHANGES BETWEEN RAVI ZACHARIAS AND LORI ANNE THOMPSON

R avi Zacharias has never denied the authenticity of his suicide email and he quotes from this email chain in his federal complaint. The email addresses for the Thompsons have been altered to protect their privacy. Ravi's was made a matter of public record by his attorneys, and his ministry did not reply when I asked if they objected to my including it here.

From: Lori Anne Thompson
<loriannethompson@*.*>
Date: October 29, 2016 at 1:04:58 PM EDT
To: Ravi <rakzach@gmail.com>
Subject: Letter

Dear Ravi,
I can no longer continue, even in the seams of my soul, tuck away what I know to be sin against God and each of our spouses. Sin as you know always divides and devours. I cannot however continue to live with myself, with the guilt and shame that I feel about what has happened.

In order to move forward with my spouse, I am planning on telling him what has happened tonight. The cost of this has been staggeringly high, and I have no idea if my marriage will be salvaged. All I can do is beg his forgiveness and try to heal so that something of this nature never happens again. Please do to reply, as I simply cannot hear from you or see you ever again. I have no control over how Brad will respond to or handle the information but I can no longer hold this secret and its soul searing shame.

Let me say I have three daughters Hannah, Samantha and Abigail. If one of my daughters was approached by a man thirty years her senior in a position of power and trust, and this type of thing had occurred, I would be furious with him. I suspect so would you if it were one of your precious girls.

You sir, are that man. You took advantage of a devastated daughter, and left her devoured once again. I am so appalled that I allowed myself to enter into this level of deception. You took and I gave a part of my soul and later my body that was not yours. The investment in relationship from taking my email to taking off my clothes makes me weep with the despair; feeling desolate, devastated, and disgusted.

As for always, I recant on a vow I cannot keep. It is only He that will be with me always.

Lori Anne

———

From: Ravi rakzach@gmail.com
Date: October 29, 2016 at 4:38:00 PM EDT
To: Lori Anne Thompson
<loriannethompson@*.*>
Subject: Re: Letter

Are you going to tell him it's me?

———

From: Ravi <rakzach@gmail.com>
Date: October 29, 2016 at 4:38:48 PM EDT
To: Lori Anne Thompson
<loriannethompson@*.*>
Subject: Re: Letter

You promised you wouldn't Lori Anne. If. You betray me here I will have no option but to bid this world goodbye

I promise

———

From: Ravi <rakzach@gmail.com>
Date: October 29, 2016 at 5:03:34 PM EDT
To: Lori Anne Thompson
<loriannethompson@*.*>
Subject: Re: Letter

Can we not meet at lest once before you do this?

Please please

———

From: Ravi <rakzach@gmail.com>
Date: October 29, 2016 at 5:57:00 PM EDT
To: Lori Anne Thompson
<loriannethompson@*.*>
Subject: Re: Letter

Little did I know that was the most dark and accursed day of my life. You will not hear from me again

———

From: Lori Anne Thompson
<loriannethompson@*.*>
Date: October 29, 2016 at 6:15:42 PM EDT
To: Ravi <rakzach@gmail.com>
Subject: Re: Letter

We are Lori Anne's counsellors and she is currently re-ceiving intensive counselling with us to find healing and restoration for her marriage. It is not her intent to share what has happened to anyone except her husband--which is necessary for any hope of marital restoration. And we are bound by confidentiality. We need some assurance from you that you will not harm yourself. Otherwise, we will find it necessary to contact 911 in your location. We await your prompt response. Thank you.

———

From: Ravi <rakzach@gmail.com>
Date: October 29, 2016 at 6:18:08 PM EDT
To: Lori Anne Thompson
<loriannethompson@*.*>
Subject: Re: Letter

I am fine Thank you. I am just concerned about her.
Thank you please tell her I am praying for her. She is
very much in my prayers

Brad had wrote an email from my icloud account with one word
"Apology?" I did not keep that email... this was Ravi's response.

From: Ravi <rakzach@gmail.com>
Date: November 15, 2016 at 2:47:26 AM EST
To: Lori Anne Thompson
<loriannethompson@*.*>

That's the only way as a follower of Jesus. Yes. Even
though the love of life has gone and hangs on by a
slender thread. Heaven is more beautiful each day.
In the land of my birth. Memories of youth and childhood....

God be with you and your beautiful family

From: Brad & Lori Anne Thompson
Date: November 17, 2016 at 10:41:31 AM EST
To: <bradkthompson@*.*>
Subject: From Lori Anne

Please forward to Ravi on my behalf. I would be grateful.

Dear Ravi,

I have spent countless hours trying to comb through
the annals of my soul and spirit trying to dissect ana-
tomically what has happened. What I let happen, what
I didn't see coming and why. What you meant to me,

how that played out, what to do with that now and so on...

If I could go back, I'd run to no less than a thousand moments. I can't. I cannot rewrite history, and perhaps that is a good thing. What I can say with integrity is that I loved you with a pureness of heart despite how things shifted. I wanted then and ardently want now - your best and highest. I failed Brad, I failed you, I failed God and myself.

I have struggled lifelong with a deep and profound sense of shame. This has added to it immensely. I will process this for a long time to come.

I wish for you to assume the very best of me, despite my failure; I will assume the very best of you. I will cover you with a blanket of mercy now and always and ask that you do the same for me.

I have not been able to pray for you until last night. Something broke through last night to permit me to do so once again.

In His grace,

Lori Anne

I cannot express enough my wish for restoration for you especially your heart as I too am a man just like you who has lived to long in his head. Sincerest Blessings

Brad

On Nov 17, 2016, at 8:36 PM, Ravi <rakzach@gmail. com> wrote:

Thank you to you both. The heart is broken and only the Lord can heal. The tears roll and only the Lord can wipe away. I promise to be a better man.

I have informed my office that I will turn in my phone next week. Ten years ago before email etc life gave me more time to read and spend with my lord. I know with

travel this poses greater risks not to give me access-
especially in the middle east. But God protected me
over all those years. He will do so in the future.

Thank you for your prayers. That means a lot to me. I
need it. Those prayers will carry me. With my prayers

Ravi

(don't know if you heard of the chaos in India right now
with the demonetization shock. can't change money
anywhere. We are trying to head home. Never seen
anything like this in my travels

From: Brad Thompson <bradkthompson@*.*>
Date: November 18, 2016 at 7:36:35 AM EST
To: Ravi <rakzach@gmail.com>
Subject: Re: From Both of Us.

O dear God Ravi. Please don't promise to be better.
I (Lori Anne) laid on the bed heart broken and wept
when I read that bit. You have said it twice. Once to
each of us. It was the grief of God that overtook me.

We can't be better. Can you not see God right beside
us? He is at your right hand.

It is no coincidence that you are in India right now. It
is no coincidence that the demonitorization in India
is happening at this moment I (brad) beseech you to
understand...

That which is counterfeit has flooded the financial mar-
kets, and as such is of no value. Even that which is not
counterfeit has become valueless.... that which is real
is rendered worthless.

You are likely the most powerful Indian man globally
who has both a platform and a meaningful message.
It is counterfeit to think that being better is the answer.
All sons of India, you and your nation holds this belief
falsely not just in the head, but deep into its very heart.

That is why the striving, the jumping off buildings, the culture of shame, the searching, sacrificing and hungering for literally millions of deities. Even their gods compete against one another in a spiritual one-up-manship.

Can you imagine your kids or grandkids coming to you and saying this... "Papa, I'll let myself know and be known when I become better, sin less and perform more. I will make myself more acceptable to you." Noooooooo!!!!!

The Father alone says this....

You are beloved as your birthright. You are my son...

this knowledge MUST travel the long and arduous distance from your head to your heart.

You, your family, your nation and millions of Christians all over the world are literally starving for the message of a Father who loves you and wants your heart in the deepest of places.

Your MOMENTARY failure is safe with us, we assume ours is safe with you.

We love you. I, Brad, love you. You, we, were created for such a time as this. All creation is sitting on the edge of its seat waiting to see the Sons of God revealed. Christ in you and in me. Brothers of the same father.

Let us each walk the rest of our lives in an effort to "wipe the face of our earthly father off the face of God." You are accepted. You are acceptable.

Our deepest corporate prayer this day, the one we both believe is His prayer for you is that you may never do better. That you may move from doing to being...

being broken, being intimate, being authentic, being vulnerable, being spacious, being tender, being accepted.

Know that I (Brad) am standing on Gods shoulders with my hands in the air cheering you on. Finish well my dear friend, in His strength, on the wind of His passionate love for you and His endless favour bestowed on your being.

In His Grace,

Brad and Lori Anne

PS - We will be sending you a small gift at Christmas. Don't be alarmed when you see the package. It will be a gift of grace.

Sent from my iPhone

_____

From: Ravi <rakzach@gmail.com>
Date: November 18, 2016 at 11:25:00 AM EST
To: Brad Thompson <bradkthompson@*.*>
Subject: Re: From Both of Us.

My dear Brad and Lori Anne

I received your message a couple of hours ago and I kid you not, like Pilgrim of old I felt the burden I had carried, roll down as he ascended the hill with the Cross on it. I truly sobbed my heart out when I read your last paragraph, Brad. That is the most incredible thing to read- that you would be cheering me on.... we sing so much about Grace but there is nothing like being on the receiving end when it is a pure gift and completely undeserved by the recipient. Then to add the even greater touch....that song of being no longer afraid...

I had never heard it too, till last Sunday when I preached in London at Hillsong. My heart almost burst out of me praying then that the day would come. Now here it is.

There is no such thing as clean air in India, but I had to take a walk after receiving your beautiful letter- from both of you- and not a soul knew that as I walked a crowded and messy sidewalk, in the dark, dodging traffic each time I had to get on to the side of the road--

that God had just returned in my heart with unspeakable Joy.

Incredibly, the song that kept me weighed down for days was

"Where is the joy that once I knew When first I saw the lord

Where is the soul's refreshing view of Jesus and his word

What peaceful hours I once enjoyed How sweet their memory still

But they have left an aching void This world can never fill."

For the life of me I had never thought of that song for years because it is so morbid. Lo and behold, the enemy of our souls kept those words coming back in my mind.

Now, two lines erased that completely:

"No longer a slave to fear

I am a child of God."

I can still hear the worship team singing it, now as you bring it to mind. The grand weaver has done His weaving with a confluence of His mercy.

You know the Indian culture well, Brad. I'm amazed how well you see through the weight of their faith and reactions. This is how we are raised. Shame, guilt, superstition, you must pay, and hence the karmic law. Today I saw the lines outside the banks and the pushing and shoving. I didn't even dare go within twenty yards of the crowds. A stampede could have broken out. It's all so insane.

But that is how a culture without Grace and hope, lives.

What you both have said and written embodies our faith in clearer tones than I have ever seen lived out. Thank you for living out our Lord's message in a way the world can never understand, until sin and Grace meet and Grace wins it all. Wesley said it beautifully:

"T'was Grace that taught my heart to fear and Grace my fears relieved."

Whatever your Christmas gift is, I am overwhelmed at the thought, but what you have demonstrated exceeds any gift that can come...

I retire to sleep now with a heart overflowing with a fresh touch from above. May His word be even more powerful than ever before. Thank you for for your trust. Maybe in heaven we will be together and see in full measure how beautiful this gift of God has been through deep waters to a glorious Rescue.

I leave for Mumbai tomorrow to speak to an almost completely Muslim and Hindu audience- it is the mother Theresa award for a young Muslim gunned down saving his friends. Imagine that- they have asked me to bring the message of Jesus to this audience. I am praying for wisdom.

God bless you dear Brad and God bless you dear Lori Anne.

You both are loved in a way words cannot describe. Ravi

From: Priscilla David <P.org>
Date: November 29, 2016 at 2:24:32 PM EST
To: "lthompson" <lthompson@*.*>
Subject: Surprise :) :)

Dear Lori,

Greetings to you from Atlanta, GA. How are you doing my friend? It has only taken me over 2 months and 2 days to write to you L L I have remembered you several times and prayed for you. How are things at your end especially in your family? Do write to me when you have a few minutes and please let me know how else I can cover you in prayer. I would really like to do that.

Much love to you dear sister.

Warm regards and blessings,

P

Communications Assistant to the President

_____

From: BT
Date: December 5, 2016 at 12:28:23 PM EST
To: Ravi <rakzach@gmail.com>
Subject: Re pictures

Ravi, this is Brad

I will cut to the chase.

I too am a man as my wife has shared with you. I have forgiven you, my wife, and myself.

I am looking for an assurance that the photos that were sent to you by Lori Anne where she was clothed and nude are no longer in your possession and have been destroyed. I believe you would want the same assurance and honesty if I had received intimate pictures of one of your daughters.

LA told me she had sent a similar request for assurance and not heard back from you. I know you have received and responded to my earlier emails at this address. I await your honest response. Brad

Sent from my iPhone

_____

From: Ravi <rakzach@gmail.com>
Date: December 5, 2016 at 5:44:49 PM EST
To: Brad Thompson <bradkthompson@*.*>

Subject: Re: Re pictures

My dear Brad

This is Ravi I am in Seoul Korea on the last trip before my Christmas break. I hope you are all well.

I am sorry that you had to even ask that. May I assure you both that every picture has been deleted and was done so immediately. That is both my promise and assurance. Never kept a single one of them. I was sure I had stated that. They were destroyed within seconds.

That is my deepest assurance to you and Lori Anne. Actually I even promptly delete messages both personal and official because I travel so much in case my phone is ever lost or stolen.

As I mentioned, I will be giving up the use of a cell phone shattering this one and therefore unlocatable or unusable to self or anyone. One of the reasons I erase at the end of each day is just in case people try to hurt my family with the life threats that the Islamic world makes on me and my family. And as a traveling man, life is always uncertain. The phone will be totally unusable and information irretrievable to anyone. Once again, as for pictures and messages. All were erased and never shared. I double checked each time that they were permanently gone. I commit to you, Brad. I am sorry that you even had to ask again. It was and is a given.

Thank you once again for your heart oof Grace and love. I am always in your debt as a gift from God. What happened then will never happen again.

A blessed Christmas to you. That song "I am a child of God" is permanently playing in my mind. And seems to come up on many a program I am part of. With gratitude

Ravi

APPENDIX 3: DEMAND LETTER
TO RAVI ZACHARIAS

BRYANT
LAW CENTER P.S.C.
BRYANT • SHANNON • ROARK

April 27, 2017

Mark P. Bryant
Wm. Kevin Shannon
Emily Ward Roark
Joe B. Roark
N. Austin Kennady
Samantha Bussey

Of Counsel: Albert Jones

Personal and Extremely Confidential

Mr. Ravi Zacharias
780 Buttercup Trace
Alpharetta, GA 30222
rakzach@gmail.com

Mr. Zacharias,

I am writing you on behalf of my clients, Lori Anne and Brad Thompson, citizens of Belleville, Ontario, Canada, both followers of yours, supporters of your ministry, and two people who believed you could do no wrong. Both of them were very much under your influence. They were thrilled with the opportunity to meet you in person at the Businessman's Luncheon in Kingston, in 2014. Little did they know that day when your assistant specifically requested the contact information from Lori Anne that she would become the object of a grooming process that lasted for months as you gained her trust as a spiritual guide, confidante, and notable Christian statesman. In that position you were obligated as a Christian and by law to engage with this couple with the utmost integrity. With your ongoing encouragement, Lori Anne Thompson was made to feel safe with you in the confines of a confidential relationship. As a result of your actions, she eventually opened up her life to you to the point where you exercised a controlling influence over her as one with spiritual authority. Armed with that information and your excellent grooming skills, you chose to exploit her vulnerability to satisfy your own sexual desires. Not only did you engage in sexually explicit online conversations, but you also solicited and ultimately received many indecent photos of Lori Anne throughout the course of your communications with her. Your selfish and predatory behavior has caused irreparable harm to the Thompson family from which they may never recover.

In an email following many lengthy telephone conversations with you (we have copies of your emails and the call register), Lori Anne informed you of her decision to tell Brad about this misconduct. You responded by email that you would end your life and "bid this world goodbye" if she confessed and outed you to her husband. You later admitted that this was not true and we have independent confirmation of many of these discussions by an anonymous third party.

Your appalling actions have had and will continue to have heartbreaking consequences for the Thompson family. Brad and Lori Anne are in therapy and marriage counseling and both have been unable to work more than part time since Lori Anne disclosed this nightmare to Brad. Brad has attempted to take his life and remains suicidal, while Lori Anne is medicated for post-traumatic stress and anxiety. The eldest child who knows what happened has been devastated on so many levels and is struggling to make sense of it all.   In short, your reprehensible actions have destroyed their marriage and left their home in shambles.

Mr. Zacharias, we can proceed with this matter in either of two ways:

1.   You can notify your Board of Directors and all of your insurance carriers for your ministry, your professional coverage and your homeowners insurance of pending litigation. If that is the path you choose, you are hereby on notice as of this date to take affirmative steps to prevent anyone with access to your data, systems and archives from seeking to modify, destroy or hide electronic evidence on personal or business cell phones, tablets or laptops, networks or local hard drives. Our client, Lori Anne Thompson, while under your guidance and at your request provided you with multiple images of herself in the nude, the receipt of which you have acknowledged in communications which we possess. You are further instructed to retain any documents or other tangible evidence relating in any way to the Thompsons or any other individuals with whom you may have carried on an inappropriate relationships arising out of your role as a spiritual leader. If you fail to preserve and maintain this evidence, we will seek any sanctions available against you and your company under Georgia law. R.A. Siegel Co. v. Bowen, 246 Ga. App. 177, 539 S.E.2d 873 (2000).

2.   In the alternative of protracted and public litigation, the Thompsons will sign a release of you and your church and ministry in exchange for a certified check in the amount of $5 million dollars made payable to the Bryant Law Center, Lori Anne Thompson and Bradley Thompson within thirty days of today's date, and mailed to the above address. DO NOT contact or attempt to contact my clients. I will not talk to you but will speak to your attorney should he wish to call me.

I trust you will govern yourself accordingly.

Sincerely,

BRYANT LAW CENTER, P.S.C.

Mark P. Bryant
Attorney-At-Law

Enclosure

109

APPENDIX 4: RZIM PRESS RELEASE REGARDING RAVI'S CREDENTIALS

RZIM: Statement on Ravi Zacharias' Biography
Posted by Ruth Malhotra on December 3, 2017

The veracity of some of the educational credentials—specifically the use of the "doctorate" designation—of our Founder and President, Ravi Zacharias, have been called into question. While Ravi personally does not brandish his credentials and routinely asks not to be referred to as "Dr. Zacharias"—even by employees—our organization bears his name and, as such, we would like to take this opportunity to clear up any misunderstanding.

Neither Ravi Zacharias nor Ravi Zacharias International Ministries (RZIM) has ever knowingly misstated or misrepresented Ravi's credentials. When it has been brought to our attention that something was stated incorrectly with regard to Ravi's background, we have made every effort to correct it. Sometimes other entities—such as publishers or institutions where Ravi was speaking—have incorrectly presented aspects of his credentials. We were not aware of these errors when they were made; however, in some instances RZIM should have caught them and sought to have them corrected. We regret any and all errors, as well as any doubt or distraction they may have caused.

Currently, eleven RZIM team members have earned doctorates. Ravi is not one of them, nor has he ever claimed to have an earned doctorate.

In fact, Ravi often states that he wishes he had done more formal studies, as he values and understands the importance of higher learning. Ravi has a Masters of Divinity from Trinity International University, and has also been conferred with ten honorary doctorates. Ravi is grateful for and humbled by where the Lord has taken him during his 45 years of ministry thus far.

In earlier years, "Dr." did appear before Ravi's name in some of our materials, including on our website, which is an appropriate and acceptable practice with honorary doctorates. However, because this practice can be contentious in certain circles, we no longer use it.

In addition, some confusion may have arisen from a difference in cultural norms, as we are a global organization with staff members based in sixteen countries. In Ravi's homeland of India, for example, honorific titles are customary and are used frequently out of respect for elders, including by the RZIM India team when addressing Ravi. Still, it is Ravi's custom to request for the inviting parties not to use "Dr." with his name in conjunction with any speaking events. Despite this, on occasion it has been our experience that we arrive to find promotional banners and materials welcoming "Dr. Ravi Zacharias." We will continue to do our best to ensure consistency; however, we recognize that certain aspects are sometimes beyond our control.

The nature of our work at RZIM can evoke criticism, sometimes fair—in which case we address it—but sometimes completely unfounded and without merit. For example, recently a couple of inquirers claimed to have information that Ravi was facing discipline from his denomination. This is simply false and has never been the case, and it serves as an example of why we choose not to address certain accusations that come our way.

We will be more vigilant about editing and fact-checking at every stage. Our hope is that this will enable us to focus on our primary calling of helping people to encounter the claims and person of Jesus Christ, and will enable others to focus on the strength and merit of our message.

Ravi's desire and our desire as an evangelistic ministry is to engage the honest skeptic, to take questions seriously, and to be as clear as possible in our communication. We therefore have restructured Ravi's biography to better reflect his 45 years as an itinerant evangelist and apologist with a passion and a calling to reach those who shape the ideas of culture with the beauty and credibility of the gospel.

APPENDIX 5: RAVI ZACHARIAS'S PRESS RELEASE ON HIS FEDERAL LAWSUIT

Ravi Zacharias: Statement on My Federal Lawsuit
Posted by Ravi Zacharias on December 3, 2017

In October 2014, I spoke at a conference in Canada. At the conclusion of my talk, I met a couple who expressed an interest in our ministry. The wife asked if I would reach out to her husband because he had questions about the Christian faith. As requested, I followed up by sending an email and a book to him, and invited him to consider attending one of our educational programs at Ravi Zacharias International Ministries (RZIM).

Some months later, I traveled with my wife and one of our daughters to another part of Canada for a speaking engagement. The couple attended this event and invited my wife and me to dinner at a local restaurant afterwards. That was the second and last time I was ever in the same room with either of them.

Subsequently, she began to contact me via the email address I had used to contact her husband after first meeting them. My responses were usually brief. Then, last year, she shockingly sent me extremely inappropriate pictures of herself unsolicited. I clearly instructed her to stop contacting me in any form; I blocked her messages, and I resolved to terminate all contact with her.

In late 2016, she sent an email informing me she planned to tell her husband about the inappropriate pictures she had sent and to claim that I had solicited them. In April 2017, together they sent me, through an attorney, a letter demanding money. I immediately notified members of my board, and as they advised, I personally engaged legal counsel.

In response to the demand for money, my attorneys filed a publicly available lawsuit under the Racketeer Influenced and Corrupt Organizations Act (RICO). The other side requested mediation rather than going to trial. We agreed to mediation and we reached an agreement in November 2017 to resolve the matter and dismiss my lawsuit. All communication with both of them has concluded, and the legal matters have been resolved. However, at this time, unfortunately I am legally prevented from answering or even discussing the questions and claims being made by some, other than to say that each side paid for their own legal expenses and no ministry funds were used.

I have learned a difficult and painful lesson through this ordeal. As a husband, father, grandfather, and leader of a Christian ministry I should not have engaged in ongoing communication with a woman other than my wife. I failed to exercise wise caution and to protect myself from even the appearance of impropriety, and for that I am profoundly sorry. I have acknowledged this to my Lord, my wife, my children, our ministry board, and my colleagues.

Let me state categorically that I never met this woman alone, publicly or privately. The question is not whether I solicited or sent any illicit photos or messages to another woman—I did not, and there is no evidence to the contrary—but rather, whether I should have been a willing participant in any extended communication with a woman not my wife. The answer, I can unequivocally say, is no, and I fully accept responsibility. In all my correspondence with thousands of people in 45 years of ministry, I have never been confronted with a situation such as this, and God and my family and close friends know how grieved I have been.

In my 45 years of marriage to Margie, I have never engaged in any inappropriate behavior of any kind. I love my wife with all my heart and have been absolutely faithful to her these more than 16,000 days of marriage, and have exercised extreme caution in my daily life and travels, as everyone who knows me is aware. I have long made it my practice not to be alone with a woman other than Margie and our daughters—not in a car, a restaurant, or anywhere else. Upon reflection, I now realize that the physical safeguards I have long practiced to protect my integrity should have extended to include digital communications safeguards. I believe— and indeed would counsel others—that the standards of personal conduct are necessarily higher for Christian leaders.

The Lord rescued me at the age of seventeen, and I promised to leave no stone unturned in my pursuit of truth. He entrusted me with this calling, it is His; any opportunities I have been given are from Him. My life is not my own, it belongs to God. As long as He gives me life and breath I will serve out this calling He has given me. I am committed to finishing well, using whatever years He grants me to share His love and forgiveness, truth and grace, with people everywhere who are looking for meaning and purpose and hope. I bear no ill will toward anybody. God is the God of healing, and He promises a new day. May that be true by His grace.

APPENDIX 6: MINISTRYWATCH INVESTIGATIVE REPORT ON RAVI ZACHARIAS (REPRINTED WITH THE KIND PERMISSION OF MINISTRYWATCH)

Ravi Zacharias Faces Criticism for Exaggerated Credentials and Settling a Lawsuit with an Apparent Extortionist
November 27, 2017

R avi Zacharias International Ministries (RZIM), a well-respected teaching ministry in evangelical circles with a global reach, has recently been criticized by a self-proclaimed atheist who has devoted considerable time and energy to discrediting many of Ravi Zacharias' claimed academic credentials. His name is Steve Baughman and he describes why he has focused on Ravi Zacharias on his website (see http://www.raviwatch.com/about/ for his detailed description of how he came to critique him).

Baughman focused initially on the various academic credentials Ravi Zacharias claimed. He noted while Zacharias referred to himself as Dr. Zacharias, the only doctorates he has received were honorary doctorates.

COVER-UP IN THE KINGDOM

In responding to a request for a comment on this issue, RZIM provided the following explanation:

> *The convention on honorary doctorates varies from institution to institution, but the degree is often conferred in recognition of an individual's contribution to a particular field. Furthermore, one can use the title without claiming that it is an earned academic degree.*

MinistryWatch has learned there is no set convention on whether it is appropriate for someone who has received an honorary doctorate to refer to themselves as "Doctor". Given the academic nature and depth of Zacharias' teaching ministry, his referring to himself as "Dr. Zacharias" does not seem inappropriate to us at MinsitryWatch.com. Nevertheless, the ministry no longer refers to Zacharias as "Dr." Zacharias.

Baughman goes on to dissect a variety of Zacharias' other academic claims and his research is thorough. You can find it fully described on his website (http://www.raviwatch.com/documentation/). In reviewing this research and the response from the ministry about it, it is our view Baughman does reveal an unfortunate pattern of Zacharias, at a minimum, exaggerating his academic background. While we do not believe this determination in any way undermines the excellent teaching material that RZIM has produced over the years, we took note of it in case additional information ever arose which would indicate these exaggerations had begun to reveal a more consequential character issue at RZIM. Unfortunately, new information has arisen which does raise hard questions for donors to RZIM, but there are not many good answers to those questions and it now appears there may never be any.

Recently, Baughman highlighted a court filing by Ravi Zacharias in relation to an apparent extortion attempt against himself. To quickly summarize a complex situation, a married couple posing as potential donors to RZIM allegedly sought to put Zacharias in a compromised position by having the wife provide nude photographs of herself to Zacharias via e-mail and/or text message. The couple then had a lawyer draft a letter asking for a $5 million payment to prevent disclosure of the matter to the public. Ravi Zacharias (personally, not the ministry) responded with a civil complaint against the couple. We would urge RZIM donors to read the letter to RZIM from the couple's lawyer and the civil complaint filed by Ravi Zacharias. It certainly seems to be a pretty straightforward extortion attempt against Ravi Zacharias. The couple has a history of using litigation against a previous pastor of theirs to gain financial remuneration for an alleged financial scheme that had gone bad. Additionally, RZIM provided MinistryWatch with the following written response to our inquiries about this news:

> *Thank you for your inquiry. The lawsuit filed by Ravi Zacharias is a response against a Canadian couple that has made egregious false claims against him and have attempted to extort a large sum of money from him based upon meritless allegations.*
>
> *Ravi Zacharias will vigorously defend himself against these harmful mistruths and extortion attempt. It is our prayer that these false allegations will stop, but because previous actions by the couple have indicated that may not be possible, Ravi Zacharias will seek all available remedies in the legal system.*
>
> *Since this a legal matter, we are not at liberty to speak further about it. However, Ravi Zacharias has always maintained a high level of personal and professional integrity. False accusations against his personal character and biblical leadership are not a matter he takes lightly, and his decision to pursue legal action was made only after thorough prayer and consideration.*

Upon our following up with more specific questions generated from the evidence he provided in his court filing, RZIM provided this further written statement:

We understand your questions and appreciate you reaching out to RZIM for context. Since Ravi's federal lawsuit against the Thompsons is currently being litigated in Court, we have to allow the legal process to disclose all the evidence in the filing, which limits how much we can discuss with other parties.

We do, however, stand by our claim that the Thompsons are unjustly attempting to extort money from Ravi and that he has not had any inappropriate activity with Ms. Thomson online or otherwise, including never meeting privately with her or soliciting photos from her. I can also confirm that our board stands unanimously with Ravi Zacharias; affirms his character and integrity; and fully supports his decision to move forward with a lawsuit against the Thompsons for harassing him.

Unfortunately, this is yet another example of people hostile to the Gospel and the stand the organization has taken on certain issues, who want to specifically discredit and mislead others about Ravi Zacharias.

At RZIM, we will continue to follow Jesus' commands to pursue holiness and proclaim the life-giving message of Christ in diverse arenas. We are confident that God will guide us at each step, praying that the truth will be revealed and hopeful that His name will be glorified as He reveals his redemptive purpose.

Thank you again for your expressed concerns; I hope this helps explain the situation.

We subsequently asked RZIM if the ministry's board of directors, which includes Zacharias' wife and daughter, had seen copies of the e-mail and text communications sent between Ravi and the alleged extortionists, as this would give us greater confidence the board's strong backing of him was based on the information and evidence we would like to see, but cannot. RZIM's response indicated the board has not yet seen the e-mail and text evidence that would support Zacharias' claims in his court filing but had been "briefed" about it. Of course, the alleged extortionists have also not provided such evidence either. Here is the response we received from RZIM:

> *As I mentioned in my last email, the RZIM Board of Directors is completely supportive of Ravi as he pursues the truth in regards to these false allegations of which they have been briefed.*

In our view, the principal issue in this case is whether Zacharias solicited the nude photos or not. The couple naturally claims he did. Zacharias, of course, claims he did not and neither side has yet provided evidence to support their case. So it is a classic "he said, she said" case. One charge by the alleged extortionists which Zacharias did not refute in his filing, however, was that Zacharias threatened to commit suicide if the woman told her husband about their online relationship. We doubt the absence of a rebuttal to this charge was an oversight by Zacharias or his lawyers and it suggests the alleged extortionists do have some evidence to back at least this one claim up. While this is disconcerting, as it seems to imply some guilt on Zacharias' part, it seems appropriate to give the benefit of the doubt to Zacharias rather than a couple with a litigious history seeking a $5 million extortion payment from him.

Even so, Zacharias' own explanation in his court filing of how this situation developed over a period of two years raises questions about his judgment in this matter. He allowed a professional relationship with a prospective donor couple to develop into an online friendship with just the wife. This led to the woman giving Zacharias exercise advice for his bad back including photos of her apparently performing the exercises. These photos apparently progressed from normal photos to scantily clad pictures to eventually nude snapshots. It is hard to see how Zacharias allowed this progression to occur although he claims to have sought to block her messages to him and to cut off all communication with the woman. Nevertheless, communications at some level clearly continued and the filing does not offer an explanation as to how or why this happened. Nor did Zacharias attempt to involve his board of directors in this situation at an early stage of its development, allowing the situation to escalate. And RZIM is not willing to share any additional details to address the concerns we raised about how Ravi handled this unfortunate extortion attempt. We have asked why the court filing did not include more evidence of Zacharias' e-mails or text messages to the woman that would back up his case about not soliciting the pictures as well as other matters, but RZIM stated they could not respond due to the case being in the courts at that time. The only evidence of an e-mail from Zacharias to the alleged extortionists included in Zacharias' court filing was an edited e-mail to the woman's husband which seems to include an admission of Zacharias' guilt regarding letting an online relationship with the woman go too far while simultaneously denying he ever requested nude photos. Here is that section of Zacharias' court filing:

> Specifically, on January 24, 2017 (Plaintiff's {Zacharias} last direct communication with the Thompsons {Alleged Extortionists}), Plaintiff sent an e-mail to Mr. Thompson that stated, in part:

> "Let me answer your question as best as I can without risk of seeming to avoid the full force of the responsibility. Whatever the reason the blame is real and inescapable. But to answer your question--I can say from my conscious that I never initiated or proposed that action . . . . Once that came about I can also say that I repeatedly made every effort not let [sic] it continue and suggested that I even block my mail, which I did. Each time I asked for no further contact, agreement was made [sic], and never once did I ever initiate it again . . . . By the way, with the determination to not continue what was wrong, I purposely never met her even once. When she paid a visit to Atlanta for other reasons, I deliberately was out of town . . . ."

On November 9th, however, the case was settled without going before a judge and/or jury and therefore, we may now never get answers to the questions that naturally arise from that which we do know at this point. As part of the settlement, all parties to the suit are governed by a non-disclosure agreement (NDA) which means none of the parties to the case can comment on any aspect of it to the public. This is unfortunate as it leaves a cloud of uncertainty over the ministry. Using NDA's in cases like this are essentially a way for the guilty to make sure their mistakes are covered up. The only reason we can see why Zacharias would settle this case before It went to trial and use an NDA is that the trial would bring out damaging evidence against him. If Zacharias had evidence which would prove those seeking to extort money from him were lying, it is hard to imagine he would not pursue this even if the legal costs were high. It was our sincere hope the legal process would completely exonerate Zacharias and MinistryWatch delayed sharing anything about this case for months on the hope evidence would be presented clearing Zacharias. Due to the settlement, which one can only presume was achieved by Zaharias person-ally paying the alleged extortionists some sum of money, it now appears clear he was likely guilty of something in this situation which would cause him significant reputational damage, above that which is already known about this case, had it become public. At the same time, it needs to be remembered his alleged extortionists also never presented evidence to confirm such misbehavior on his part (naturally, since if they made the information they had public, there would be no reason for Zacharias to pay them for their silence) and their background and actions in this case easily leads one to question their truthfulness. Still, the onus is on Ravi Zacharias to more fully explain what actually occurred. Outside of one helpful call from a RZIM UK board member (a separate legal organization than RZIM US), RZIM has only communicated with us via e-mail and has often not answered many of the questions we have asked, claiming they could not do so because the matter was before the court. Most of those questions were also posed before the NDA was in place. As noted earlier, RZIM claimed in their e-mails that Zacharias was going to fight this extortion attempt "vigorously", but then Zacharias settled the case before it went to trial where RZIM's assertions of the "false claims" made against Zacharias could have been proven to indeed be false. One can reasonably conclude, therefore, the couple extorting Zacharias actually did indeed have damaging e-mails and texts from him.

While RZIM has stated to us the ministry made no payments in the settlement of the case (presumably any payments made to the alleged extortionists came directly from Ravi Zacharias), they did not answer our question if Zacharias has received any unusual compensation from the ministry recently which may have assisted him in making payments to settle the case.

Meanwhile, while quite disturbing, none of the above undermines the solid, biblically-based teaching for which RZIM and Ravi Zacharias have become well-known around the world. In MinistryWatch's view, the ministry's teaching materials are excellent and the roughly 80 RZIM staff traveling the world to share this teaching are very effective. However, both the credentials exaggeration issue and the unfortunate online relationship with the couple, which led to their seemingly successful extortion attempt of Zacharias, raise legitimate questions about Zacharias' character and judgment. In MinistryWatch's opinion, these troubling developments are significant enough to warrant making donors to RZIM aware of this situation.

In situations like this, donors look to the ministry's board of directors to take appropriate actions to protect both the ministry and donors. We have been told the board of RZIM has instituted new policies in an effort to protect against any reoccurrence of such problems. Leaders at RZIM, including Zacharias, we have been told will now be provided with traveling companions to provide additional accountability and protection for them (similar to Billy Graham's longstanding practice) and the ministry has made increased efforts to make sure all biographies of its leaders are those approved by the ministry for accuracy. The ministry has also shared a new policy document describing how staff should respond to situations similar to what the founder recently faced so that they can be dealt with immediately. While these steps are helpful, the RZIM board should also examine its own response to these developments as they originally offered a strong statement that the claims made by the alleged extortionists were false when we were told they had actually only been "briefed" on the situation and had not yet seen any evidence which would exonerate Zacharias.

Now that the case has been settled while employing the legal tactic of an NDA to prevent any further evidence from being made public, it seems the board of RZIM may have too quickly rushed to defend their ministry's founder and perhaps misguided others in the process. Indeed, the RZIM board may now be in the same uncomfortable position as everyone else interested in the success of the ministry as they too are unable to see the evidence necessary to determine the full extent of the predicament Ravi Zacharias got himself into.

APPENDIX 7: RAVI'S OFFICIAL BIO FROM BEFORE THE CREDENTIAL SCANDAL

This is Ravi's official bio as it appeared immediately before his credential scandal went public. His ministry later claimed that Ravi has resisted the title "Dr." but we see here that he used it eight times. The misleading Cambridge and Oxford claims have also since disappeared from his official bio. I have bolded and italicized the notable examples in this reproduction.

Ravi Zacharias is Founder and President of Ravi Zacharias International Ministries (RZIM), which celebrated its thirtieth anniversary in 2014. ***Dr.*** Zacharias has spoken all over the world for 42 years in scores of universities, notably Harvard, Dartmouth, Johns Hopkins, and Oxford University. He has addressed writers of the peace accord in South Africa, the president's cabinet and parliament in Peru, and military officers at the Lenin Military Academy and the Center for Geopolitical Strategy in Moscow. At the invitation of the President of Nigeria, he addressed delegates at the First Annual Prayer Breakfast for African Leaders held in Mozambique.

Dr. Zacharias has direct contact with key leaders, senators, congressmen, and governors who consult him on an ongoing basis. He has addressed the Florida Legislature and the Governor's Prayer Breakfast in Texas, and has twice spoken at the Annual Prayer Breakfast at the United Nations in New York, which marks the beginning of the UN General Assembly each year. As the 2008 Honorary Chairman of the National Day of Prayer, he gave addresses at the White House, the Pentagon, and The Cannon House.

He has had the privilege of addressing the National Prayer Breakfasts in the seats of government in Ottawa, Canada, and London, England, and speaking at the CIA in Washington, DC.

Dr. Zacharias was born in India in 1946 and immigrated to Canada with his family twenty years later. While pursuing a career in business management, his interest in theology grew; subsequently, he pursued this study during his undergraduate education. He received his Master of Divinity from Trinity International University in Deerfield, Illinois. Well-versed in the disciplines of comparative religions, cults, and philosophy, he held the chair of Evangelism and Contemporary Thought at Alliance Theological Seminary for three and a half years. Dr. Zacharias has been honored by the conferring of a Doctor of Divinity from four institutions: Houghton College, Tyndale College and Seminary, McMaster Divinity College, Toronto, and Trinity College of Florida. He has also been honored with a Doctor of Laws degree from Asbury College, Kentucky, and a Doctor of Sacred Theology from Liberty University, Virginia. He is presently Senior Research Fellow at Wycliffe Hall, Oxford University in Oxford, England.

Dr. Zacharias has been a *visiting scholar at Cambridge University*, where he studied moralist philosophers and literature of the Romantic era. While at Cambridge he also authored his first book, *A Shattered Visage,* updated and republished in 2004 by Baker as *The Real Face of Atheism.* His second book, *Can Man Live without God* (Word, 1994), was awarded the Gold Medallion for best book in the category of doctrine and theology, and *Jesus Among Other Gods* (Word, 2000) was nominated for a Gold Medallion. Several of his books have been translated into Russian, Chinese, Korean, Thai, Spanish, and other languages. In all, *Dr.* Zacharias has authored or edited well over twenty books, including *Why Jesus?* (FaithWords: 2012), *Has Christianity Failed You?* (Zondervan, 2010), *The Grand Weaver* (Zondervan, 2007), and *Beyond Opinion* (Thomas Nelson, 2007), which includes contributions from RZIM's global team. His latest books are a graphic novel version of *The Lamb and the*

Fuhrer (Kingstone Media: June 2014) and *Why Suffering?*, coauthored with Vince Vitale and released by FaithWords in October 2014.

At the invitation of Billy Graham, *Dr.* Zacharias was a plenary speaker at the International Conference for Itinerant Evangelists in Amsterdam in 1983, 1986, and 2000. He is listed as a distinguished lecturer with the Staley Foundation and has appeared on CNN, Fox, and other international broadcasts. His weekly radio program, "Let My People Think," airs on 2087 outlets worldwide; his weekday program, "Just Thinking," on 706; and his one-minute "Just a Thought," on 414. Various broadcasts are also translated into Romanian and Turkish, and "Let My People Think" airs as the Spanish-language program "Pensemos" on over 250 outlets in seventeen countries. Additionally, his television program, "Let My People Think," is broadcast internationally in several countries including Indonesia.

RZIM is headquartered in Atlanta, Georgia, with additional offices in Canada, India, Singapore, the United Kingdom, the Middle East, Hong Kong, Romania, Turkey, Austria, Spain, and South Africa. *Dr.* Zacharias and his wife, Margie, have three grown children. They reside in Atlanta.

APPENDIX 8: MY PERSONAL AGENDA

"Singing works just fine for me." – James Taylor

Ravi Zacharias defenders almost always ask me about my motives. Rarely do they ask about my message.

In my fantasies I tell them that I am on a mission from Satan to destroy a powerful Man of God who is lowering Hell's occupancy rate. But, I tell them, here's the catch; my Master commands that everything I say about Ravi be true. My Master may be a really bad guy, but he wants to win fair and square, not by making stuff up, as more reputable folks so often do.

There! We are clear about the messenger. Can we now look at the message?

That would be hoping for too much. As one who suffered much during my own faith transition away from evangelical Christianity I think I have an inkling into what may be going on in the minds of the most ardent Ravi defenders.[263] It is not something that can be shaken off with a dose of reason, for reason cannot usually rescue people from situations that reason did not get them into in the first place. I loosely paraphrase Sam Harris when I say that religious believers have a lot at stake; if their religion is false much, if not all, is lost. At the very least they won't see their deceased child/parents/spouse in heaven. A similar dynamic is at work in the minds of many of Ravi's most enthusiastic defenders. The wisdom and sincerity of Ravi Zacharias is the thread by which hang their hopes for eternal life. If it turns out that Ravi is a scoundrel, their religion is false. If you think this is an overstatement, I encourage you to spend an hour or so reading the venomous and irrational social media posts of Ravi defenders. These are people for whom much more is at stake than the integrity of some smiling preacher.[264]

It is also much easier to dismiss a bearer of bad news as ill-motivated than it is to plow through emails from the University of Cambridge Office of External Affairs and Communications. Not only is the latter kind of boring, but if you stay awake until the end you'll see that Ravi really did lie, and from this there follow the aforementioned theological consequences. Hence the resistance.[265]

There is nothing I can do about those people. But you got this far in the book, so you may be different. Perhaps you will take heed as I put Master Lucifer (or was it Satan? Are they different?) aside for a bit and tell you what really moves me here.

Christian missionaries were my heroes growing up in Southeast Asia. These folks lived for a mysterious intangible that seemed to me far more worthy than the international business success that motivated my crowd. Whatever that something was, they shunned my comfortable expat community and dwelled in the *kampongs* where they could share that intangible with the locals. And they didn't need words to tell us that dark skin was as precious in God's eyes as any.

When I moved to the United States at age 18 I joined a Southern Baptist church and became active in my campus InterVarsity group. They welcomed me, perhaps because I was an exotic kid who rode his bicycle on the freeway and had no idea who the Stones were.

After a couple of years, I faith transitioned, but the missionaries remained my heroes even after I concluded that their religion was probably false. My respect for the institutions that had trained, supported and nurtured these heroes also survived. Say what we will about their politics and their theology, these organizations were made up of love-filled people who would lay down their lives for their principles. My belief in God's people survived my loss of belief in God.

Then I encountered Ravi Zacharias.

It was early 2015 and, as you may recall from an earlier chapter, I was on my usual search for the best and brightest defenders of the Christian religion that I could find. Anyone who takes an intellectual search seriously needs to find and engage the most qualified people we don't agree with, even though it is way more fun to beat up on the dumb folks. And if these smart opponents have multiple doctorates and hold academic appointments at Cambridge and Oxford, well, they may still turn out to be wrong, but the fact that they know vastly more than I do makes dismissing them a hard to justify move. After all, they come highly recommended by an intellectual community that holds its members to the extraordinarily rigorous standards that caused me to take a terminal M.A. at U.C. Berkeley and drop academia as a career path. I knew I could not keep up intellectually with the world of serious academic scholarship. (Law school turned out to be much easier.)

Simply put, when I encounter philosophical opponents who have reached intellectual heights that I may never even hope for, I feel called to epistemic humility. How presumptuous it would be for me to dismiss their greater minds as wrong when I know they would beat me up in any debate, public or private. How intellectually dishonest! Even worse, how cowardly! It reeks of the false bravado of calling the neighborhood bully a cissy when he is not around.

Unfortunately for those who decide to hold themselves to high standards of epistemic integrity, they may never be entitled to feel comfortable with their beliefs. That is just the way honest searches works. The truth does not care what is important to you, and it will never seek you out to guide you in all things. If you have intellectual integrity you may just have to make your peace with never really knowing what religion, if any, is true. Even the greatest Christian philosophers can't close the case for their precious religious beliefs.[266]

If I told all this to my psychoanalyst s/he would tell me that my motives in outing Ravi Zacharias have nothing to do with my allegiance to Satan. I just resent the hell out of Ravi because I have the courage to admit that I can never be a first-rate scholar with Oxford and Cambridge credentials and I have no hope of ever acquiring the expertise to discern exactly which version of which religion is the one and only true one. By the starkest of contrasts, Ravi happily (or at least smilingly) pretends that he has all that. And he gets away with it.

Well, Ravi gets away with it sometimes. He fooled me for a brief bit. I first encountered him in a YouTube lecture he gave to some students at the University of Illinois. He made a slam dunk argument for God's existence based on fulfilled prophecy in the Book of Daniel.

I was thoroughly moved, ready to adjust my worldview if this panned out. And it seemed likely to. Ravi was no Hal Lindsey/Josh McDowell hack. I wasn't quite sure who he was, but the fact that he was a Cambridge and Oxford scholar with several doctorates was enough to shift the burden to me. Burden accepted. "Until further notice, please be advised that this atheist is now an agnostic."

Ravi initially made that happen for me by presenting the Book of Daniel as an uncontroversial 6th century B.C.E. document. Since it described Alexander the Great to a tee centuries before he existed it had to be prophetic.

I looked into the claim. Ravi, it turns out, had misled the audience. Daniel was written two centuries years *after* Alexander. No wonder it predicted him so well.

Ravi and I had dinner together in Burlingame, CA, a couple years after I had decided he was a scoundrel. During our all too brief conversation he persuaded me that maybe his Daniel argument had not been so dishonest. Daniel, he told me, was prophetic even on the later dating because the book predicted things that transpired *after* the alleged late date.

Fair enough. Ravi scored points with me here. But that only proved that God exists.[267] More significant for present purposes is that Ravi's Daniel argument, right or wrong, got me looking into who Ravi Zacharias really was. And what I found changed my view not only of Ravi, but of the massive religious business complex that enables him

It was not so much that Ravi was a scoundrel. Ravi Zacharias was just one guy. My sobering up came with the discovery that the institutions that nurtured my missionary heroes were equally adept at promoting people like Ravi Zacharias. As I shared my Ravi findings with those in the God business, I met with precisely the sort of behavior exhibited by the embattled tobacco companies, Catholic bishops, and politicians caught with their pants down. The response, usually delivered with the help of P.R. professionals, was denial, deceit, evasion, counterattack, with carefully crafted *mea culpas* issuing only when the denials had stopped working.

Exposing Ravi Zacharias may seem like a big part of why I wrote this book. But I have a far greater concern. Ravi will be leaving us in a few years. And despite his life's work, skepticism about religion is on the rise worldwide.[268] With atheism's newfound respectability we see increasingly sophisticated debates between religious and non-religious scholars. This fantastically rich dialogue is, I think, much needed. But healthy debate and competition in the marketplace of ideas require that nobody participate under false pretenses. Ravi Zacharias has been a shameful imposter in these debates, dumbing down the issues in ways that his audiences, blinded by his impeccable scholarly credentials, miss. Christian business leaders have been his shameful joiners.

It is my hope that this book will encourage the Christian business world to bring its ethical standards in line with those that its counterparts in the secular world, my world, have agreed to abide by. Only when this happens can we have a fair contest.

Whether this happens or not will be up to John Lennox, Jeremy Begbie, Margaret Manning Shull, Abdu Murray, Amy Orr-Ewing, the

C&MA, the Southern Baptist Convention, the Brunson Boys, Ruth Malhotra, Ligonier Ministries, the folks at HarperCollins Christian like Casey Harrell and Dan Foutz, and all those in the God business who so love the status quo.

Karl Marx would predict that God, Inc. will keep doing business with Ravi Zacharias as long as the bottom line warrants it. It is one thing, after all, for Christians to love God. It is quite another for them to love God more than they love profits.

If it turns out that the Christian God really exists, we atheists will not be the only ones in trouble on Judgment Day. God, Inc. does not seem worried. Nor am I.

APPENDIX 9: IF RAVI ZACHARIAS BELIEVED IN GOD

TO RZIM SUPPORTERS AND DONORS AND TO ALL WHO HAVE TRUSTED ME:

As the leader of an international concern bearing my name, I have frequently consulted lawyers and public relations professionals on matters of import to my career and my public image. The time has now come for me to listen to my heart. A still, small voice has long reminded me that, in the words of G.K. Chesterton, "The Christian ideal has not been tried and found wanting. It has been found difficult; and left untried." Although these words have resounded in my heart with clarity and urgency, I would not hear them. Now I must.

Throughout my career as a credentialed minister of the gospel I have allowed my passion for the message of Christ to blur my vision of what it means truly to follow Him. So eager have I been to win souls for the Kingdom that I overlooked the fact that my Lord never asked me to deceive others in my Christian service.

Though my motives were pure, I now repent of my systematic practice of overstating my academic credentials in the service of the gospel. Against the advice of my business colleagues and long-time reputation advisors I make the following confession.

I never held a formal position at the University of Oxford and I was never a professor or an "official lecturer" there. I was never a "visiting scholar at Cambridge University," nor did I study quantum physics at that institution. My claims to the contrary were false.

My claim to having been "educated in Cambridge" was intended to create a false impression of my academic qualifications. My claims to having chaired a department at Alliance Theological Seminary and to having won an international preaching competition in 1965 were also false.

For over three decades I deliberately misled the public into believing I have earned several doctoral degrees. I not only routinely failed to disclose that my doctoral degrees were merely honorary, but I also deliberately employed ambiguous language in my promotional materials to create the impression that mine were academic doctorates. When my deceptions were made public in a way that was irrefutable, I permitted my ministry in December of 2017 to issue a misleading press release implying that I have resisted being called "Dr. Zacharias." The truth is that I have actively promoted myself as "Dr. Zacharias" since the early 1980s.

In my book, *The Real Face of Atheism*, I wrote "Nothing is as important as the truth." I deeply regret my career-long failure to behave as though I believed this.

Some may question the motivation behind my confession, which comes only after my falsehoods were exposed in ways that my reputation professionals, despite their best efforts, were unable to neutralize. To demonstrate the sincerity of my repentance, I have asked the publisher of my memoirs, *Walking from East to West*, in which I made many of these false claims, to discontinue the book. I have also informed this publisher, HarperCollins Christian Publishing, that I wish to be released from my contractual obligation to write the book *Jesus through Eastern Eyes*, which is slated for publication in 2020.

Now is not the time for business as usual, but for me to commence a period of focused self-reflection, contemplation and prayer.

I must confess also that my relationship with Lori Anne Thompson was more involved, intimate and mutual than I disclosed in my federal lawsuit and press statements. It is a testament to the magnificent power of the blood of Christ that I, a career minister of the gospel, may find forgiveness for threatening suicide to prevent a struggling Christian woman from taking steps to heal her marriage. It was, perhaps, an even greater sin that I allowed my lawyers to employ a legal strategy that would save my reputation by falsely tarnishing hers and that of her husband. Whether or not the Thompsons are ever able to forgive me, I am profoundly and humbly thankful for the blessed assurance that, by this confession, my Lord has.

Ravi Zacharias
Christmas Eve, 2018
Alpharetta, GA.

N.B.: As of the date *Cover-Up in the Kingdom* enters production, Ravi Zacharias has not made this confession.

NOTES

1   Excerpted from *Beyond Opinion: Living the Faith We Defend* (Thomas Nelson, 2007), ed. by Ravi Zacharias, back cover.

2   See, for instance, *The Real Face of Atheism* where he releases two birds from one cage with pro-truth quotes from Chesterton and himself. Ravi Zacharias, *The Real Face of Atheism* (Grand Rapids, Michigan: Baker Books, 2004), 105.
For a pro-truth tweet from Ravi, see: Ravi Zacharias (@RaviZacharias), "Truth cannot be sacrificed at the altar of pretended tolerance," December 1, 2016, accessed October 7, 2018, https://twitter.com/ravizacharias/status/804522323369787393.
Or just Google "Ravi and truth" for evidence that the apologist cares deeply about getting his facts right.

3   Ravi Zacharias, "How Wide the Divide: Sexuality at the Forefront, Culture at the Crossroads," RZIM (blog), July 15, 2015, accessed October 7, 2018, https://rzim.org/global-blog/how-wide-the-divide-sexuality-at-the-forefront-culture-at-the-crossroads.

4   Kate Shellnutt and Sarah Eekhoff Zylstra, "Ravi Zacharias Responds to Sexting Allegations, Credentials Critique," *Christianity Today*, December 3, 2017, accessed October 6, 2018, https://www.christianitytoday.com/news/2017/december/ravi-zacharias-sexting-extortion-lawsuit-doctorate-bio-rzim.html.

5   See, for instance, the statement from the Southern Evangelical Seminary spokesperson in Chapter 10.

6   Ravi Zacharias, *Beyond Opinion: Living the Faith We Defend* (Nashville, Tennessee: Thomas Nelson, 2010), on back cover.

7   This was Prison Fellowship founder Chuck Colson's description of Ravi. Dick Staub, "Ravi Zacharias's Wonderful World," *Christianity Today*, January 1, 2004, accessed October 6, 2018, https://www.christianitytoday.com/ct/2004/januaryweb-only/1-12-22.0.html.

8   The email exchange is at Appendix 2.

9   I replied as follows: "You may want to let them know that these materials are with multiple sources now and whatever happens to me or my sources will just encourage others to publicize forth with" [sic]. I received no reply.

10   Evangelical Council for Financial Accountability, "Ravi Zacharias International Ministries," accessed September 7, 2018, http://www.ecfa.org/ComparativeFinancialData.aspx?ID=9175&Type=Member.

11   The claim appears to have disappeared from Ravi's website. It is preserved here at 14:15: Steve Baughman, *Lying for Lord or Self? Hard Questions for Ravi Zacharias*, YouTube video, accessed October 5, 2018.

12   Ravi Zacharias, *Walking from East to West: God in the Shadows* (Grand Rapids, Michigan: Zondervan, 2010), 199.

13   Motoko Rich, "Gang Memoir, Turning Page, Is Pure Fiction," *New York Times*, March 4, 2008, accessed October 6, 2018, https://www.nytimes.com/2008/03/04/books/04fake.html.

14   Jana Brubaker, *Text, Lies and Cataloging: Ethical Treatment of Deceptive Works in the Library* (Jefferson, North Carolina: McFarland), 67.

15   Peter Hessler, "What Mortenson Got Wrong," *New Yorker*, April 21, 2011, accessed October 6, 2018, https://www.newyorker.com/news/newsdesk/what-mortenson-got-wrong.

16   Theologian John Stackhouse put it mildly when he complained of the "long and not very edifying tradition of Christian evangelists and speakers inflating their credentials." https://www.facebook.com/john.g.stackhouse/posts/10154771955516612. And again, "I've been worried for 20 years about someone finally doing exactly this," Facebook, November 23, 2017, accessed August 7, 2018,

17   Ravi's federal complaint (hereafter "Complaint") at paragraph 22. The complaint can be viewed at www.RaviWatch.com and at the court's PACER system online.

18   I have been torn about whether to include a photo of Lori Anne Thompson in this book. In weighing her privacy interest against what I take to be the newsworthiness of her image, I have split the baby and produced a photo of her from over a decade ago. Lori Anne includes current photos of herself at her blog and twitter account, which, as I note later, are worth visiting for insight into the genuineness of her concerns about clergy abuse.

19 Complaint, paragraph 36.

20 Ravi denies requesting the photos but, as we shall see, the case against him is strong.

21 I have included the email exchanges as Appendix 2.

22 Appendix 2.

23 Robert McKee, "True character is revealed in the choices a human being makes under pressure," GoodReads Quotable Quotes, accessed September 9, 2018, https://www.goodreads.com/quotes/647959-true-character-is-revealed-in-the-choices-a-human-being. From *Story: Substance, Structure, Style, and the Principles of Screenwriting* (New York: Harper-Collins, 2010).

24 Appendix 2.

25 Appendix 2.

26 Appendix 2.

27 Appendix 2.

28 Appendix 2.

29 I have reproduced this letter at Appendix 3.

30 *Walking*, 38.

31 *Walking*, 71.

32 *Walking*, 82.

33 *Walking*, 94.

34 *Walking*, 33.

35 "About Ravi Zacharias," Wayback Machine, accessed August 26, 2018, https://web.archive.org/web/20150424065544/http://rzim.org:80/about/ravi-zacharias.

36 *Walking*, 115.

37 Early in his career he was often billed as "the Billy Graham of India" in his promotional materials. *Tampa Times*, July 27, 1974, 10.

38 *Walking*, 18–19.

39 *Walking*, 40.

40 For a better sense of Ravi's celebrity fetish, see the *Philippine Daily Inquirer* article about the opulent wedding of two Filipino celebrities that Ravi officiated in Paris on September 2, 2017:

Nikko Tuazon, Angelique Sampayan, and Karen Caliwara, "Did the

Vicki Belo–Hayden Kho Jr. Wedding Cost P80 Million?", *Philippine Daily Inquirer*, September 6, 2017, accessed September 11, 2018, https://www.pep.ph/lifestyle/celebrations/36041/did-the-vicki-belo-hayden-kho-jr-parisian-wedding-cost-p80-million.

It appears that Ravi made a special trip to Paris for the star-studded event that is estimated to have cost over $3 million: accessed September 11, 2018, https://rzim.org/bio/ravi-zacharias/#/?i=3.

41 *Walking*, 99.

42 *Walking*, 101.

43 *Walking*, 107.

44 *Walking*, 102.

45 *Walking*, 103, lowercase in original.

46 *Walking* 109.

47 *Walking*, 120.

48 *Walking*, 109.

49 *Walking*, 124.

50 *Walking*, 134.

51 *Walking*, 113.

52 *Walking*, 161.

53 *Walking*, 134.

54 *Walking*, 150.

55 *Walking*, 127. Accessed September 15, 2018, https://www.zachariastrust.org/bios/ravi-zacharias.

56 Jay Kesler, phone conversation with author; Don Unger, phone conversation with author; Sam Kamaleson, email with author, summer 2017.

57 Unfortunately in the page of my interview notes memorializing this statement I failed to note which individual said this, but it would have been either Mr. Kesler or Mr. Unger since I made no notes of my email communication with Mr. Kamaleson.

58 *Walking*, 127.

59 *Walking*, 129.

60 *Walking*, 130.

61 *Walking*, 130.

62   *Walking*, 130.

63   When I met Ravi for a brief dinner in November, 2017, he promised me a letter from the contest organizer confirming this title. He has not provided that. He also told he that he had a trophy bearing the Asian Youth Preacher Award title but that it had faded. The name of the award appears in Ravi's later writings: Ravi Zacharias, "Reading: The Fingerprints on Your Soul," RZIM (blog), December 15, 2003, accessed September 15, 2018, https://rzim.org/just-thinking/reading-the-fingerprints-on-your-soul. It also appears in numerous early newspaper event announcements such as: "Asian Youth Preacher Award," *Madison Eagle*, April 7, 1983, accessed September 15, 2018, https://www.newspapers.com/image/244415950/?terms=%22asian%2Byouth%2Bpreacher%2Baward%22.

Those wishing to search further may get a free trial subscription from Newspaper.com to verify my claim that the "Asian Youth Preacher Award" is a Ravi Zacharias invention. Or simply Google the prize.

64   *Walking*, 133.

65   *Walking*, 156.

66   *Walking*, 193.

67   *Walking*, 208.

68   There actually was no Canadian ambassador to India, but, rather, a High Commissioner.

69   *Walking*, 141.

70   *Walking*, 142.

71   Conrad Hackett, "By 2050, India to have world's largest populations of Hindus and Muslims," Pew Research Center, April 21, 2015, accessed August 21, 2018, http://www.pewresearch.org/fact-tank/2015/04/21/by-2050-india-to-have-worlds-largest-populations-of-hindus-and-muslims.

72   *Walking*, 142.

73   *Walking*, 156.

74   *Walking*, 157.

75   *Walking*, 185.

76   Alexander Oppong-Mensah at Trinity Evangelical Divinity School, personal email with author, September 19, 2016.

77   I am also unable to find evidence that he has ever published a scholarly paper nor presented his work to a scholarly conference.

78   See, for instance, his dramatic account of taking the atheist Cambridge professor Don Cuppitt down a few notches. *Walking*, 205–06.

79   With some bravado Ravi tells us that his studies "inspired me with the confidence to walk into any lion's den and believe I would come away victorious for the gospel" (*Walking*, 175). That confidence may have since waned. In June, 2018, I tried to arrange a debate between Ravi and the atheist Richard Carrier, an historian with a doctorate from Colombia. I offered Ravi convenient terms and said he could choose the moderator. His ministry, through Ms. Penny Howard, promptly replied that while "[i]n the early years Ravi did do some debates…he does not consider that approach to be of greatest value, which is why he prefers to do Open Forums." His ministry then said "He would recommend one of his colleagues, such as John Lennox or Abdu Murray, who are the debaters on the team." I found two things interesting in this email. First, I do not believe Ravi has *ever* engaged in a formal debate. After a fairly extensive search, the closest thing I have found is a panel discussion of two Christians and two non-Christians. Ravi's Christian partner was William Lane Craig, the respected apologist and scholar with two PhDs. I followed up with RZIM several times to request confirmation of what seems to be their false claim about Ravi's earlier debates. Despite their prompt reply to my debate offer, they ignored my several inquiries about Ravi's prior debates. The second thing that struck me was that while Ravi does not find debates "to be of greatest value," (per Penny Howard)he regularly has his RZIM evangelists do them. While one can understand some people not seeing debate as a productive use of their skills, Ravi's reluctance suggests he is like the magician who can only do his tricks in a dimly lit room because light saps his magical powers. Ravi's "Open Forums" are conducive to his verbal sleight of hand. A face-to-face encounter with a worthy opponent would shine too much light on his methods. This, I suspect, is why he refuses to do them. (Penny Howard at RZIM, email to author, June 4, 2018.)

80   *Walking*, 185.

81   I believe that he founded the center and made himself its chair. However, the Seminary's embargo on Ravi Zacharias information, which we will discuss shortly, has made it difficult for me to confirm this.

82   Dennis Hollinger, now president of Gordon-Conwell Theological Seminary, phone call with author. Another of those who described Ravi's center as an "informal" undertaking was Kerry Bowman, now a somewhat influential minister in Southern California whom Ravi describes as one of his "closest friends" from the ATS years (*Walking*, 189–90). Pastor

Bowman was a student of Ravi's at ATS in the 1980s. In May 2017 I spoke with him at length, and he told me that he was now studying for his doctorate of divinity. This surprised me because his LinkedIn profile showed that he had completed his doctorate at Fuller Theological Seminary the year before we spoke. He explained to me that the LinkedIn entry was a mistake, and I believe him. But I then noticed that he had taken his ATS master of divinity and described it as a "master's degree, evangelism and contemporary thought." Pastor Bowman was doing exactly what his seminary teacher, Ravi Zacharias, did. He reworded his titles to make them seem more academic. I have no desire to cast Kerry Bowman as a dishonest man. But at the very least he is a willing participant in an evangelical Christian culture that sees credential enhancement as its birthright.

83   The earliest reference to the "department" that I can find is in *The News Journal* (Wilmington, Delaware), December 4, 1982, 34, accessed September 15, 2018, https://www.newspapers.com/search/#query=%22department+of+evangelism+and+contemporary+thought%22. See also *Walking* at p.188.

84   Terry Wardle, phone call with author, May 24, 2017, and Dennis Hollinger, phone call with author, May 26, 2018. Both were professors at ATS in the 1980s. Dr. Hollinger was there during Ravi's time and Dr. Wardle came in 1985 just after Ravi had left. My private investigator in New York went to the seminary and reviewed school catalogues with the assistance of the librarian. He found no indication of departments at ATS. The seminary itself refused to answer my repeated question as to whether it had ever had departments.

85   *The Journal News* (White Plains, New York), November 28, 1981, 8.

86   Karen Davie, email with author, May 4, 2017.

87   Karen Davie, email with author, May 4, 2017. I also received a copy of this page in the catalogue from my private investigator.

88   Walter Sevastian, email with author, May 16, 2017.

89   *Walking*, 195–96.

90   There are, of course, privacy rights that an employee has, and I do not suggest that the C&MA simply make Ravi's personnel file public. But the church could demand that Ravi acknowledge the false and misleading claims he has made about his job at their seminary.

91   Shellnutt and Zylstra, "Ravi Zacharias Responds to Sexting Allegations."

92   The Associated Press Stylebook put the common sense approach to

honorary doctorates like this: **honorary degrees** — All references to an honorary degree should specify that the degree is honorary; honorary degrees are not earned through a degree-granting academic program of study. Do not use *Dr.* before the name of a person whose only doctoral degree is honorary.

Those wishing to see the proper and honest use of honorary doctorates by a legitimate scholar may peruse atheist philosopher Daniel Dennett's curriculum vitae at http://ase.tufts.edu/cogstud/dennett/cv.html accessed 9/24/18.

93   Per Ravi's C.V. posted at RZIM.org, https://rzim.org/wp-content/uploads/2018/01/Ravi-K-Zacharias-CV.pdf accessed 9/8/18.

94   I have included copies of some of his early ads in the photo section of this book. Ravi's defenders have sometimes argued that everybody knows that the Doctor of Divinity is an honorary degree. Houghton College, for instance, the Christian college that gave Ravi his first honorary doctorate, told me that "a D.D. is by definition an honorary degree. . ." (personal email communication with Houghton's P.R. Specialist, Michelle Hillman, 8/28/18.) But not only does not everybody know that, it happens to be false. The folks behind the Wikipedia entry, for instance, do not know it. They refer to the D.D. as "an advanced or honorary academic degree in divinity." https://en.wikipedia.org/wiki/Doctor_of_Divinity accessed 9/8/18. FreeDictionary.com refers to it as "a doctor's degree in religion." https://www.thefreedictionary.com/Doctor+of+Divinity accessed 9/8/18. The University of Oxford, where Ravi long claimed to be a professor, describes a rigorous and expensive application process that a candidate seeking the D.D. must go through, including demonstrating "an original contribution to the advancement of theological knowledge" such as to give the candidate "an authoritative status in this branch of learning." https://www.admin.ox.ac.uk/examregs/2014-15/doctofdivi/ accessed 9/8/18. A quick google search of the degree shows various seminaries in the United States offering earned D.D. degrees. In any event, it is difficult to think of anything other than dishonesty to explain Ravi's failure to simply put "Hon." in his promotional materials.

95   See for instance the back cover of his 2008 book, *New Birth or Rebirth?*, published by Multnomah Books. "Zacharias holds three doctoral degrees."

96   Thanks to the Wayback Machine these claims are preserved. https://web.archive.org/web/20150424072345/http://rzim.org:80/bio/ravi-zacharias accessed 9/8/18. I have also reproduced Ravi's 2015 bio as Appendix 7.

97   *Walking*, 190.

98   In Ravi's event announcements as far back as 1980 he fails to follow the convention of stating using "(Hon)" in his title. See https://www.newspapers.com/search/#query=%22dr.+ravi+zacharias%22&offset=155 accessed 10/1/18.

99   https://ca.rzim.org/about/ravi-zacharias/ accessed 9/15/18.

100 See https://mse.osu.edu/defense-dissertation accessed 8/22/18.

101 Reprinted in its entirety by *Christianity Today*, "Ravi Zacharias Responds to Sexting Allegations, Credentials Critique" December 3, 2017, at https://www.christianitytoday.com/news/2017/december/ravi-zacharias-sexting-extortion-lawsuit-doctorate-bio-rzim.html accessed 9/8/18.

102 There is a study to be done here, both quantitative and qualitative. Do evangelical males abuse themselves more in this regard than others do? Do they crave pedigree enlargements more than other males do? If so, why? I considering it a promising hypothesis that, due to the very technical nature of apologetics, professional Christian evangelists see the need to have extensive graduate level academic training in philosophy and theology. Those who lack such education, which is most apologists, are aware of their deficiency. By putting "Dr." in front of their name they subtly diminish their own sense of inadequacy and make it less likely that others will notice that they are pretenders. This theory explains why "Dr." appears so frequently on the signs outside of churches and so rarely on the signs outside other businesses. We see the same phenomenon in another field marked by a similar professional insecurity; chiropractors regularly market themselves as "Dr. John Smith, D.C.," a peculiar redundancy that is best explained by a need to convince others that they really are real doctors. Really, they really are. By contrast, most lawyers in the United States, members of a profession not known for its self-doubting ways, are doctors of jurisprudence but do not flaunt the title in any way. (Then there are those who have doctorates and *do* flaunt them, like the C&MA pastor who calls himself the "Rev. Dr. David M. Berman, Th.D." http://clfchurch.com/church-leadership/ accessed 9/8/18.)

103 "RZIM: Statement on Ravi Zacharias' Biography" reprinted at Appendix 4 and viewable at https://rzim.org/global-blog/rzim-statement-on-ravi-zacharias-biography/ accessed 8/21/18. The press release Ravi also made the following more general claim, "Neither Ravi Zacharias nor Ravi Zacharias International Ministries (RZIM) has ever knowingly misstated or misrepresented Ravi's credentials."

104 The complaints came from me.

105 These RZIM website changes can be viewed at the Wayback Machine. The Machine did not capture enough information from the OCCA (Ravi's apologetics school in the city of Oxford) website to establish my claim. Fortunately, I took my own screenshot in June of 2016 of the OCCA website, which had then recently added "honorary" to Ravi's bio. They took it down soon after, and this change is reflected in the Wayback Machine's next entry of May of 2017. All of this information, of course, is available from RZIM and the OCCA directly, and they have no non-deceptive reason for refusing to share it, nor for explaining why "honorary" was removed and at whose request.

106 "Ravi Zacharias Sermons Update - Who is God," at 30:20, published 1/12/18 at https://by.ytube.org/video/PvdLhQ3Mz04 accessed 10/10/18.

107 His author blurb on the back cover of *I, Isaac, Take Thee, Rebekah* (2005) says this: "Born in India and educated in Cambridge he has lectured at the world's most prominent universities as well as in more than 50 countries." https://www.christianbook.com/Christian/Books/product_slideshow?sku=908221&actual_sku=908221&slide=0 accessed 8/27/18.

108 For instance, see *Walking*, 205.

109 *Walking*, 205. There are numerous YouTube videos lectures in which he makes the claim. There is a collection of excerpts in my short video, *Ravi Zacharias Caught Lying (over and over) about Cambridge and Oxford. Two minutes of ugly evidence* at https://www.youtube.com/watch?v=povQJ6toqSg.

110 See for instance his author blurb in *Recapture the Wonder* (2005). https://www.christianbook.com/Christian/Books/product_slideshow?-sku=452767&actual_sku=452767&slide=98 accessed 8/27/18. For years he made the "visiting scholar at Cambridge University" claim at his official bio, https://web.archive.org/web/20150316211316/http://rzim.org/bio/ravi-zacharias accessed 9/24/18. A google search of "Ravi Zacharias" and "visiting scholar at Cambridge" will reveal how widely the claim has spread.

111 "Exclusive: Ravi Zacharias Apologizes for False Claims about His Credentials at Oxford and Cambridge" at https://www.wthrockmorton.com/category/ravi-zacharias/.

112 *Temple University Open Forum: Does Truth Matter?* at https://youtu.be/6-EFkOz4Pys at 15:41. Ravi calls it a semester. His supervisor at Ridley Hall, Dr. Jeremy Begbie, informed me in personal correspondence that it was 2-3 months.

113 Email communication with the University of Cambridge. "Ridley Hall is not a constituent part of the University of Cambridge and has different criteria for granting Visiting Scholar status."

114 *Walking,* 205.

115 Emphasis added. This is preserved in a 4/28/17 screenshot I made of Ravi's bio at his website. It can also be seen at https://ca.rzim.org/about/ravi-zacharias/ accessed 9/8/18.

116 Per Cambridge, the relationship between Ridley Hall and the University "is the same as it was in 1990..." (7/17/17 email from Claire Dewhurst of the University's Office of External Affairs and Communications.)

117 As of April 2018 this has been Ravi's official C.V. https://rzim.org/wp-content/uploads/2018/01/Ravi-K-Zacharias-CV.pdf accessed 8/27/18.

118 See my video "Did Ravi Zacharias really study Quantum Physics at Cambridge? Unlikely," at https://youtu.be/zV75_f_zEbU accessed10/18/18.

119 I have posted this statement at http://www.raviwatch.com/documentation/ under "The RZIM Letter to Pastor Michael Anthony."

120 Ten years later a video of Ravi's speech made the rounds on the Internet. "Living the Faith We Defend with Ravi Zacharias" at https://www.youtube.com/watch?v=vmTPxgGuA7Q&t=3148s at 52:40, accessed 10/6/18.

121 "Exclusive: Ravi Zacharias Apologizes for False Claims about His Credentials at Oxford and Cambridge" at https://www.wthrockmorton.com/2018/08/22/exclusive-ravi-zacharias-apologizes-for-false-claims-about-oxford-and-cambridge/ accessed 8/26/18

122 "Living the Faith We Defend" *with Ravi Zacharias* at 15:41 at https://www.youtube.com/watch?v=vmTPxgGuA7Q&t=3148s accessed 10/9/18. See also https://www.wthrockmorton.com/2018/08/22/exclusive-ravi-zacharias-apologizes-for-false-claims-about-oxford-and-cambridge/ accessed 8/26/18.

123 His official bio from those years is still viewable at the Wayback Machine https://web.archive.org/web/20080503205015/http://www.rzim.org:80/ravi/ accessed 9/24/18.

124 *Walking,* 229.

125 See "Lying for Lord or Self? Hard Questions" *for Ravi Zacharias* at https://www.youtube.com/watch?v=I0tbgF7U1iw accessed 10/6/18 at

5:20.

126 In June of 2015 he was still making the "senior research fellow at Oxford" claim with no hint of it being honorary. By August he had removed it. https://web.archive.org/web/20150618225520/http://rzim.org:80/about/ravi-zacharias/ (accessed 9/9/18.) It is revealing that Ravi removed all Oxford references before I even asked him about Oxford. At that point I had only notified him of my interest in Cambridge and his doctorates.

127 Personal email communication with the University of Oxford. The Oxford correspondence is preserved in my YouTube video, "Lying For Lord or Self?" at https://www.youtube.com/watch?v=I0tbgF7U1iw at 5:35, accessed 9/9/18. The same video also shows Ravi in a television interview claiming that he lectures three times a year at "Oxford University," where he is "a senior research fellow." Ravi also points out that this is where Richard Dawkins teaches. At 15:20.

128 See previous footnote.

129 Personal correspondence with the University of Oxford and Wycliffe Hall.

130 "Ravi Zacharias Interview Transcript," in Apologetics315, 2/13/13, at https://apologetics315.com/2013/02/ravi-zacharias-interview-transcript/ accessed 10/6/18. Given his lack of academic credentials or scholarly publications it is very unlikely that, despite his statement to this fellow apologist, Ravi has ever spoken at an academic forum.

131 "Exclusive: Ravi Zacharias Apologizes for False Claims about His Credentials at Oxford and Cambridge" at https://www.wthrockmorton.com/2018/08/22/exclusive-ravi-zacharias-apologizes-for-false-claims-about-oxford-and-cambridge/ accessed 9/24/18.

132 "Ravi Zacharias Responds to Sexting Allegations, Credentials Critique" 12/3/17, at

https://www.christianitytoday.com/news/2017/december/ravi-zacharias-sexting-extortion-lawsuit-doctorate-bio-rzim.html accessed 10/7/18.

133 Personal email date 6/18/15.

134 *Walking*, 205. For a video compilation of Ravi's multiple references to Cambridge and Polkinghorne see my "Ravi Zacharias Caught Lying (over and over) about Cambridge and Oxford. Two minutes of ugly evidence" at https://www.youtube.com/watch?v=povQJ6toqSg&t=2s accessed 10/1/18.

135 Emphasis added. The Begbie statement seems to have disappeared from Ravi's website, but it was preserved by Warren Throckmorton, a Christian psychology professor and Ravi critic. It can be seen in "Was

Ravi Zacharias a Visiting Scholar at Cambridge University?" at https://www.wthrockmorton.com/2017/11/28/ravi-zacharias-visiting-scholar-cambridge-university/ accessed 7/25/18. I also have a screenshot of it.

136 For years RZIM and Dr. Begbie failed to respond to my inquiries about whether Ravi had actually enrolled in classes at the University. On August 22, 2018, Ravi finally admitted that he had not. See "Exclusive: Ravi Zacharias Apologizes for False Claims about His Credentials at Oxford and Cambridge" at https://www.wthrockmorton.com/2018/08/22/exclusive-ravi-zacharias-apologizes-for-false-claims-about-oxford-and-cambridge/ accessed 8/24/18.

137 *Walking*, 205.

138 *Walking*, 206.

139 Personal correspondence from the University of Cambridge, documented in my video "Did Ravi Zacharias really study Quantum Physics at Cambridge? Unlikely."
at https://www.youtube.com/watch?v=zV75_f_zEbU&t=53s accessed 10/1/18.

140 That he merely audited is clear from his August 2018 admission to Warren Throckmorton that he never enrolled in classes at Cambridge.

141 Personal communication with Dr. Begbie. June 16, 2017. The full text of Dr. Begbie's email is here:

Dear Mr Baugham [sic]

John Polkinghorne taught courses on theology and physics for a number of years after he relinquished his full-time position in physics in the University. To my recollection, his teaching was undertaken in the Divinity Faculty at the University, and in the Federation of Theological Colleges. When Dr Zacharias spoke to me of courses in quantum physics with Dr Polkinghorne, I presume this is what he meant. I have no particular reason to doubt his claim.

I do not have the time to pursue this matter any further or in any more detail.

Sincerely,
Jeremy Begbie.

142 https://randalrauser.com/2018/09/ravi-zacharias-apologist-or-fabulist-an-interview-with-steve-baughman/ accessed 10/18/18. Dr. Rauser

told me in personal email communication that this was his first article to be rejected by the *Post*.

143   https://hamiltonstrategies.com/southern-evangelical-seminary-welcomes-ravi-zacharias-to-2018-national-conference-on-christian-apologetics/ accessed 10/15/18.

144   Dr. Land's email was shared with me by a professor at SES. I see no need to name this person.

145   Deborah Hamilton of *Hamilton Strategies*, personal email with author, October 15, 2018.

146   I have kept Dr. Lennox updated on Ravi's false Oxford and Cambridge claims through his website, http://www.johnlennox.org. He has failed to respond to several requests for comment about Ravi.

147   Dr. Lennox is perhaps the most prominent scholar at RZIM. https://rzim.org/bio/john-lennox/ accessed 9/8/18.

148   Personal communication from Dan Foutz. I also made multiple attempts to obtain comment from the senior management at HCC. I received no replies.

149   See *Ravi Zacharias and Abdu Murray bring a fresh perspective on Jesus in new book with Zondervan* at

  https://www.harpercollinschristian.com/tag/ravi-zacharias/ accessed 8/26/18.

150   *PUBLIC STATEMENT ON ACCUSATIONS AGAINST RAVI ZACHARIAS*

  https://www.cmalliance.org/news/2018/03/05/public-statement-on-accusations-against-ravi-zacharias/ accessed 8/26/18.

151   Peter Burgo, personal email with author, March 6, 2018.

152   Peter Burgo, personal email with author, March 29, 2018.

153   *MANUAL OF THE CHRISTIAN AND MISSIONARY ALLIANCE 2018 Edition* at https://www.cmalliance.org/resources/publications/manual-cma.pdf accessed 9/9/18. "The C&MA and its ecclesiastical authorities reserve the right, within their discretion, to disclose any information to outside parties as they determine appropriate under the circumstances."

154   The church's claim that it conducted "interviews with those involved" is puzzling. Did that include the Thompsons? The Thompsons were prohibited by their settlement with Ravi from discussion the matter.

The church refused to answer my question as to whether or not it had attempted to contact the Thompsons in the course of its investigations. (Personal correspondence with Peter Burgo, 9/6/18.)

155 *Defending the Faith: 2018 West Coast Conference* at https://www.ligonier.org/learn/conferences/defending-the-faith-2018-west-coast-conference/ accessed 10/7/18.

156 Personal email communication, 5/24/2018.

157 "Ravi Zacharias: Never Underestimate God," by Morgan Collier, June 13, 2018, at http://www.sbcannualmeeting.net/sbc18/news/29/ravi-zacharias--never-underestimate-god accessed August 20, 2018.

158 In personal communication Mr. Lutzweiler told me that he had contacted multiple SBC leaders to inform them about the evidence against Ravi. He had also corresponded with a "nationally known clergyman sympathetic toward the SBC" who said that Ravi had admitted to him that he had sent the suicide threat. See Chapter 15 for details.

159 https://www.baptiststandard.com/about/ accessed 8/20/18.

160 Personal email communication with Ken Camp, June 1, 2 and 4, 2018.

161 Personal communication with Jim Lutzweiler. I also sent multiple emails to Pastor Brunson and notified almost the entire pastoral staff at the Jacksonville church about the evidence against Ravi.

162 All information in this chapter about the events that transpired at the conference comes from personal telephonic and email communication with Jim. Full disclosure: I had discussed Jim's attending the conference with him prior to his attending. I paid for a portion of his expenses in making the trip.

163 Mr. Lutzweiler provided this information to me by email.

164 Trey Brunson is fiercely loyal to his father. He once tweet-bashed a pastor who left his father's church to start his own, accusing the man of "bitterness" and warning that "if a church is planted with a bitter pastor he'll lead people to bitterness." http://fbcjaxwatchdog.blogspot.com/2011/07/macs-son-trey-tweets-church-planted-by.html?m=1 accessed 9/1/18.

That day in Jacksonville he was once again doing his father's work.

165 I later learned that the Lindsay Award was largely Mac Brunson's own project. On July 18, 2018, I called the church and spoke to Lavon Rigdon, the assistant to the senior pastor. She told me that since the Brun-

sons have left there is nobody at the church who can answer my questions about the award. The Brunsons have ignored several requests from me for comment, and at least one from Warren Throckmorton. See "Christian Historian Says He Was Evicted from First Baptist Church of Jacksonville Conference Over Ravi Zacharias" 1/31/18 at

https://www.wthrockmorton.com/2018/01/31/evicted-first-baptist-church-jacksonville-ravi-zacharias/ accessed 9/9/18.

166 Complaint, opening paragraph. Ravi's federal complaint and its procedural history can be seen at the court's PACER site at https://www.pacermonitor.com/public/case/22119798/Zacharias_v_Thompson_et_al# accessed 10/6/18. I have also made the complaint available at www.RaviWatch.com. It is very likely that there were negotiations between the parties prior to the lawsuit being filed. Given the high reputational stakes for their client, Ravi's attorneys would not have ignored the April 2017 demand letter. The rush to file was probably due to the breakdown of these negotiations. But in this I speculate.

167 https://rzim.org/bio/ravi-zacharias/#/?i=3 accessed 9/11/8.

168 "Update from a War-Torn Region and Request for Prayer" at

https://rzim.org/global-blog/update-from-a-war-torn-region-and-request-for-prayer/ accessed11/6/18. Later that month his ministry posted a video of Ravi standing in a ruined church in Iraq. "Ravi Zacharias Update from Iraq" at https://www.youtube.com/watch?v=St55Ohos5qQ accessed 10/6/18.

169 You can't make this stuff up. https://rzim.org/bio/ravi-zacharias/#/?i=3 accessed 9/11/8.

170 Complaint, paragraph 98.

171 Complaint, paragraph 36.

172 Complaint, paragraph 82.

173 Complaint, paragraphs 56, 58, 59, and 64.

174 Complaint, paragraph 100.

175 This is the conclusion of *MinistryWatch*. "Ravi Zacharias Faces Criticism for Exaggerated Credentials and Settling a Lawsuit with an Apparent Extortionist "at

https://www.ministrywatch.com/articles/rzim.php accessed 10/1/18. We shall see evidence for their conclusion later in this book. The *MinistryWatch* report is also at Appendix 6.

176 Exhibit 1 to Complaint.

177 As a lawyer I am struck by the mediocre quality of the lawyering on both sides of this high-profile matter. Mark Bryant's demand letter, which he should have known could become a public record, was sloppily written, even incoherent at times. It also made his client look bad with its indelicately presented demand for $5,000,000. But the real legal blunder came when Ravi's legal team attached Mr. Bryant's demand letter to their Complaint. This Exhibit 1 made it known for the first time that Ravi had left behind an email record that proved he had made the suicide threat. Had Ravi's lawyers not added Exhibit 1 to their complaint the world may never have heard about their client's single most shocking act of misconduct. Exhibit 1 also contained unflattering and salacious descriptions of manipulation and sexual conduct that also would likely have remained a secret, and it bore Ravi's home address and personal email address, which his lawyers had not bothered to redact. Neither Mr. Bryant nor Michael Boorman (Ravi's lead lawyer) responded to my several requests for comment.

178 Complaint, paragraph 50.

179 *Walking*, 138.

180 In Prayer For Relief in the Complaint at page 35.

181 Complaint, paragraph 24.

182 Complaint, paragraph 25.

183 Complaint, paragraph 28.

184 Complaint, paragraph 29.

185 Complaint, paragraph 35.

186 "Ravi Zacharias: Statement on My Federal Lawsuit" 12/3/17 at https://rzim.org/global-blog/ravi-zacharias-statement-on-my-federal-lawsuit/ accessed 9/11/18. This is reproduced at Appendix 5.

187 Complaint, paragraph 33.

188 Complaint, paragraph 36.

189 Complaint, paragraph 37.

190 Complaint, paragraph 39.

191 Complaint, paragraph 51.

192 Complaint, paragraph 54.

193 Complaint, paragraph 56.

194 Complaint, paragraph 2.

195 Complaint, paragraph 57.

196 Complaint, paragraph 58.

197 Complaint, paragraph 41.

198 Complaint, paragraph 61.

199 Complaint, paragraph 67.

200 Complaint, paragraph 61.

201 Complaint, paragraph 75.

202 Complaint, paragraph 18.

203 Complaint, paragraph 20.

204 Complaint, paragraph 81.

205 Complaint, paragraph 82.

206 November 27, 2017 *MinistryWatch* report attached at Exhibit 6.

207 https://www.pacermonitor.com/public/case/22119798/Zacharias_v_
Thompson_et_al# accessed 10/6/18.

208 "Ravi Zacharias: Statement on My Federal Lawsuit" at https://rzim.
org/global-blog/ravi-zacharias-statement-on-my-federal-lawsuit/ accessed 9/11/18, reproduced at Appendix 5.

209 "Ravi Zacharias: Statement on My Federal Lawsuit" at https://rzim.
org/global-blog/ravi-zacharias-statement-on-my-federal-lawsuit/ accessed 9/11/18, reproduced at Appendix 5.

210 Complaint, paragraph 39.

211 Complaint, paragraphs 56, 58, 59, and 64.

212 Complaint, paragraphs 132–35.

213 Strictly speaking one need not present evidence in a complaint;
the primary purpose of a complaint is simply to state the allegations that
one intends to prove later in the litigation process. But complaints in
high-profile cases have a secondary purpose, to influence public opinion.
It is clear that Ravi's lawyers crafted their complaint with the public in
mind. Not only do they provide emails that serve their legal theory, but
their Exhibit 1 is an offer of evidence to support the extortion allegation.
As we shall see, they also included inadmissible and irrelevant material
about the Thompsons in their complaint, the only conceivable purpose of
which could have been to influence public opinion.

214 *MinistryWatch* report, Appendix 6.

215 Personal communication with Lori Anne Thompson about the birth year of their eldest child. It is possible that the "eldest child" to which Mr. Bryant refers in his demand letter is another child altogether. Still, the extortionists would have to deal with the fact that the school and medical records of that "struggling" child would be discoverable by Ravi's lawyers. If the child showed no signs of torment it would be trouble for the Thompson's theory.

216 "Rendevouses" really is a real word. https://en.wiktionary.org/wiki/rendezvous accessed 8/27/18.

217 *MinistryWatch* report. See Appendix 6.

218 "The Apologist's First Question," by Ravi Zacharias, at https://www.rzim.org/read/a-slice-of-infinity/a-living-faith accessed 10/22/18.

219 Complaint at paragraphs 65 and 72.

220 Complaint, paragraph 52.

221 Complaint, paragraph 26.

222 Complaint, paragraph 88.

223 Complaint, paragraph 55.

224 Complaint, paragraph 48,

225 Jim Lutzweiler has agreed to answer media questions about his communication with this clergyman, and I encourage interesteds to contact him about this. Credentialed media and other serious investigators may contact me for Jim's information.

226 https://spiritualsoundingboard.com/ accessed 9/11/18. I am informed that Lori Anne was also referred to and discussed her concerns with Dee Parsons, another support person and founder of The Wartburg Watch, a blog that looks at clergy abuse issues.

227 The information in this section comes from my direct communication with Julie Anne Smith. I have not seen the To Whom It May Concern letter written by Lori Anne.

228 https://twitter.com/defendthesheep/status/934123169232797696 accessed 9/11/18.

229 https://twitter.com/defendthesheep/status/937714679748616192?lang=en accessed 9/11/18.

230 This tweet is no longer available. Because it was a reply to another account user it could have been deleted. Ms. Smith is also unable to find

it. I do have a screenshot of it from 12/12/17 that I will share upon request with credentialed media.

231 Ms. Smith sent me a copy of the email she sent to the *Christianity Today* reporter. The magazine did not print her comments, although, in fairness, the comments arrived after the magazine published its one and only article, to date, about the Ravi scandals.

232 https://loriannethompson.com/

233 This is from her Twitter posts of 10/5/18.

234 See Lori Anne's post about non-disclosure agreements which I cite in our last chapter.

235 Ravi's press releases of December 3, 2017 are at Appendix 4 and 5.

236 Personal email 1/31/18. Lori Anne consistently refused to discuss her Ravi situation with me.

237 My investigator in Ontario provided me a copy of Brad's lawsuit against the pastor. Lori Anne was not a party. Ravi notes as much, but his statement that "the Thompsons" had sought money from a pastor could be misunderstood.

238 Federal Rules of Evidence sections 403 and 404.

239 'Synod 2012 Deals with Maranatha CRC and Classis Quinte' in *The Banner* 6/11/12 at

https://www.thebanner.org/news/2012/06/synod-2012-deals-with-maranatha-crc-and-classis-quinte accessed 9/11/18.

240 The 42 page report is entitled "Confidential Report. Safe Church Advisory Panel Process Report" and is dated May 31, 2013. I do not believe it is publicly available but will share it with interested credentialed media.

241 Ironically, the way Brad Thompson's litigation ended would, if anything, make the Thompsons skeptical about the ease of making money by suing clergy. Brad described the litigation to me as "troubling, lengthy, and fruitless." Personal email 7/14/18.

242 "Ravi Zacharias Responds to Sexting Allegations, Credentials Critique" in *Christianity Today* 12/3/17 at

https://www.christianitytoday.com/news/2017/december/ravi-zacharias-sexting-extortion-lawsuit-doctorate-bio-rzim.html accessed 9/11/18.

243 https://www.christianforums.com/threads/ravi-zacharias-scandal.8038090/ accessed 9/11/18.

244 *MinistryWatch* report at Appendix 6.

245 Brad's prior litigation experience with this corrupt pastor was a difficult one. As noted, he described it to me as "troubling, lengthy and fruitless." He informed me that he was eventually able recover some of his lost money, but not through litigation. (Personal email July 14, 2018.) This kind of experience with the legal process is unlikely to make anyone see abuse of the legal process as a good way to make money.

246 Email from Joe Martins of Infinity Investigations, Ontario, Canada, 8/28/18.

247 Ravi's lead attorney, Michael Boorman, has failed to respond to several requests for clarification and comment.

248 See emails at Appendix 2.

249 "How Much Does Digital Forensic Services Cost?" at https://www.vestigeltd.com/thought-leadership/digital-forensic-services-cost-guide-vestige-digital-investigations/ accessed 9/24/18.

250 *MinistryWatch* report at Appendix 6.

251 Personal email communication with Lori Anne Thompson on 2/10/18.

252 Personal email communication with Lori Anne Thompson on 7/13/18 re moving to a new city. She has tweeted about her graduate school studies. See, for instance,9/25/18 at 8:38 a.m., where she speaks of her "first grad course."

253 I gather this both from Ravi's press release and from Lori Anne's steadfast refusal to discuss the case with me despite her cordial willingness to discussing other subjects with me.

254 "Ravi Zacharias: Statement on my Federal Lawsuit." See Appendix 5 or https://ca.rzim.org/global-blog/ravi-zacharias-statement-on-my-federal-lawsuit/ accessed 8/26/18.

255 "Ravi Zacharias Responds to Sexting Allegations, Credentials Critique" in Christianity Today at https://www.christianitytoday.com/news/2017/december/ravi-zacharias-sexting-extortion-lawsuit-doctorate-bio-rzim.html accessed 10/10/18.

256 Appendix 5.

257 "Mediation can benefit the party with a 'slam dunk' case." https://www.nar.realtor/about-nar/policies/top-10-specious-reasons-why-lawyers-wont-mediate)

258 Per federal court PACER records https://www.pacermonitor.com/ public/case/22119798/Zacharias_v_Thompson_et_al# accessed 10/1/18.

259 Personal email from Lori Anne to me 1/31/18.

260 Ravi's wife has been publicly silent throughout the scandal. I suspect Margie Zacharias of being Ravi's enabler-in-chief. She was at his side when those first misleading newspaper ads started coming out in 1982 or earlier. Margie has been a loyal, silent and probably encouraging comrade to Ravi, lie after lie. But nobody deserves to feel the pain of discovering their spouse cheating on them. On this issue we owe Margie Zacharias nothing but compassion.

261 https://loriannethompson.com/2018/09/13/ndas/ accessed 10/1/18.

262 https://loriannethompson.com/2018/04/19/in-an-age-of-speaking/ accessed 8/27/18.

263 I really don't like the term "lost my faith." Why is discarding a once-dearly-held-but-untenable worldview a "loss"? I prefer "achieved liberation from my tired, false, inherited views." But it is hard to compete with the more pithy term that shall remain forever in vogue.

264 Consider this post at Dee Parson's blog, *The Wartburg Watch*, which comes from a thread about Ravi. This sincere individual has let Ravi rattle her faith. "One reason I am in a faith crisis is precisely this kind of thing: people who say they are Christian but don't even seemingly attempt to live up to the most basic of Christian ethics." From Daisy at http://thewartburgwatch.com/2017/11/29/mr-ravi-zacharias-adds-pizzazz-to-his-bio-and-the-christian-industrial-complex-imposes-the-cone-of-silence/ accessed 10/10/18.

265 In my Ravi work people sometimes accuse me of lying. But it is far more common for religious folks to simply question the coherence of any atheist criticizing anyone for any reason whatsoever. The standard line is that because we atheists have no moral grounding we thereby forfeit the right to care about anything. How can you say murder is wrong when you have no absolute standard of right and wrong? It is shoddy meta-ethics, but to evade such concerns I take pains to avoid evaluative terms like "wrong" or "evil". Instead, I limit myself to purely descriptive terms like "deceiver" and "liar" when discussing Ravi Zacharias. That so few religious believers are able to see the difference is a sad commentary on the state of religious education in the United States. And, conveniently, the focus on my philosophical incoherence obviates the need for critics to look at the evidence I produce.

266 One of my most respected contemporary Christian philosophers, Peter van Inwagen of Notre Dame, says that he needs God to help him believe. This circularity coming from such a truly brilliant mind speaks to the tension Christians face between the desire to believe and the difficulty of doing so. *God and the Philosophers: The Reconciliation of Faith and Reason* (Oxford Paperbacks) Paperback – January 11, 1996 by Thomas V. Morris (Editor) at p. 59.

267 I have since spent many hours reading about Daniel. The literature is a mind-numbing and technical hodgepodge of competing theories about the Daniel documents, which were apparently written in two different languages and at different times. To figure out the comparative virtues of the Maccabean vs Exilic dating one would need to understand the significance of the fragments found in Cave 4 at Qumran, whether or not the Aramaic is properly 6th century BCE, the significance of the fact that the book was not included in the *Nevi'im,* etc. Ravi skipped all the complexities in his speech to those undergraduates in Illinois. He simply pronounced Daniel a 6th BCE Century document, and he did so with great pizzazz, and with a great suit.

Incidentally, as part of my looking into Ravi's claim I contacted the renowned Old Testament scholar, John Collins of Yale University. Dr. Collins told me that "All mainline critics agree that Daniel was written between 167 and 164 BCE. Only fundamentalists hold to an exilic date." (Personal email correspondence, 5/27/15.) Whether Dr. Collins is right or wrong, there clearly is much controversy around the dating of the Book of Daniel. Ravi cheated his audience out of that important information.

268 "The World's Newest Major Religion: No Religion" by Gabe Bullard, *National Geographic,* 4/22/16. https://news.nationalgeographic. com/2016/04/160422-atheism-agnostic-secular-nones-rising-religion/ accessed 10/1/18.